CONTENTS

JUMBLE®

Jubilation

Euphoric Puzzles!

Henri Arnold,
Bob Lee,
Jeff Knurek, &
David L. Hoyt

TRIUMPH
BOOKS

For further information, contact:
Triumph Books LLC
814 North Franklin Street
Chicago, Illinois 60610
Phone: (312) 337-0747
www.triumphbooks.com

Printed in U.S.A.
ISBN: 978-1-62937-784-1

Design by Sue Knopf

JUMBLE®

Jubilation

Classic Puzzles

JUMBLE®

Unscramble these four Jumbles, one letter
to each square, to form four ordinary words.

BLAWR

VETEN

ULSSET

MISTEY

Amazing how you held
that pose for hours

WITH THIS KIND
OF WORK, THE MODEL
NEVER SEEMED TO
FEEL FATIGUE.

Now arrange the circled letters
to form the surprise answer, as
suggested by the above cartoon.

Print
answer
here

"⬭⬭ - ⬭⬭⬭⬭⬭⬭⬭⬭"

JUMBLE®

Unscramble these four Jumbles, one letter to each square, to form four ordinary words.

GUYLB

NUKKS

WEEYAL

SOUREA

WHAT THE CARPENTER WHO MISPLACED HIS TOOLS WAS.

Now arrange the circled letters to form the surprise answer, as suggested by the above cartoon.

Print answer here   A " ◯◯◯ " ◯◯◯◯◯◯

3

JUMBLE®

Unscramble these four Jumbles, one letter to each square, to form four ordinary words.

YUNTI

TASUE

CHUNQE

SATECK

SOME PEOPLE GET WHAT THEY WANT BECAUSE THEY HAVE THIS.

Now arrange the circled letters to form the surprise answer, as suggested by the above cartoon.

Print answer here   THE " ⬡⬡⬡⬡⬡ - ⬡⬡⬡⬡⬡⬡ "

Unscramble these four Jumbles, one letter
to each square, to form four ordinary words.

TURSY

SENWY

BINBBO

YORPET

HIS SANDWICH
ARRIVED SQUASHED
BECAUSE HE TOLD
THE WAITER TO
DO THIS.

Now arrange the circled letters
to form the surprise answer, as
suggested by the above cartoon.

*Print answer
here* " ☐☐☐☐ ☐☐ ☐☐ "

JUMBLE®

Unscramble these four Jumbles, one letter
to each square, to form four ordinary words.

WHASA

UNYTT

INDIGH

LEMITY

WHAT'S THE FIRST
THING YOU SEE AFTER
LOOKING FOR SOME-
THING IN THE DARK?

Now arrange the circled letters
to form the surprise answer, as
suggested by the above cartoon.

Print answer here

JUMBLE®

Unscramble these four Jumbles, one letter
to each square, to form four ordinary words.

JONEY

IMMAX

RUBBGY

UMSOQE

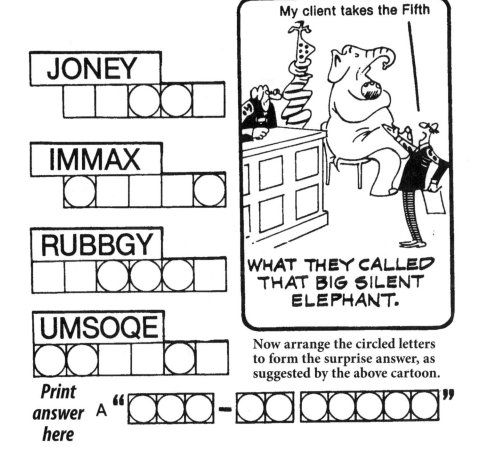

My client takes the Fifth

WHAT THEY CALLED
THAT BIG SILENT
ELEPHANT.

Now arrange the circled letters
to form the surprise answer, as
suggested by the above cartoon.

*Print
answer
here* A "⬡⬡⬡ - ⬡⬡ ⬡⬡⬡⬡⬡"

JUMBLE®

Unscramble these four Jumbles, one letter
to each square, to form four ordinary words.

UNDOP

EIDUG

DYFLON

CISEXE

WHAT HE DID
WHEN HE GOT THAT
BIG GAS BILL.

Now arrange the circled letters
to form the surprise answer, as
suggested by the above cartoon.

Print answer here

JUMBLE®

Unscramble these four Jumbles, one letter to each square, to form four ordinary words.

NAHEN

JOGIN

DINCIT

INLOPP

FOR HIM, NOTHING WAS SO DIFFICULT AS DOING THIS.

Now arrange the circled letters to form the surprise answer, as suggested by the above cartoon.

Print answer here

JUMBLE®

Unscramble these four Jumbles, one letter to each square, to form four ordinary words.

YAWNT

VAIST

RUMAID

DROWPE

THE BEST WAY TO MAKE A LONG STORY SHORT.

Now arrange the circled letters to form the surprise answer, as suggested by the above cartoon.

Print answer here

JUMBLE®

Unscramble these four Jumbles, one letter to each square, to form four ordinary words.

TUFOL

GRAWE

PANUCK

LOACCI

I know my rights!

IGNORANCE OF THE LAW IS NO EXCUSE, ESPECIALLY IF YOU'RE THIS.

Now arrange the circled letters to form the surprise answer, as suggested by the above cartoon.

Print answer here A ⬜⬜⬜⬜⬜ - ⬜⬜ - ⬜⬜⬜

JUMBLE®

Unscramble these four Jumbles, one letter to each square, to form four ordinary words.

PORDO

THECK

UCCSAU

CEETIN

SOME PEOPLE THINK THAT A KID WITH TOO MUCH SPUNK MIGHT BENEFIT FROM A LITTLE OF THIS.

Now arrange the circled letters to form the surprise answer, as suggested by the above cartoon.

Print answer here

JUMBLE®

Unscramble these four Jumbles, one letter to each square, to form four ordinary words.

MUGMY

SCAMK

VERABE

RALCOR

What he's got is the best gimmick of all

DAD

THE BEST LABOR-SAVING DEVICE.

Now arrange the circled letters to form the surprise answer, as suggested by the above cartoon.

Print answer here

JUMBLE®

Unscramble these four Jumbles, one letter to each square, to form four ordinary words.

VAROS

MURYM

TISSAD

YAIRFT

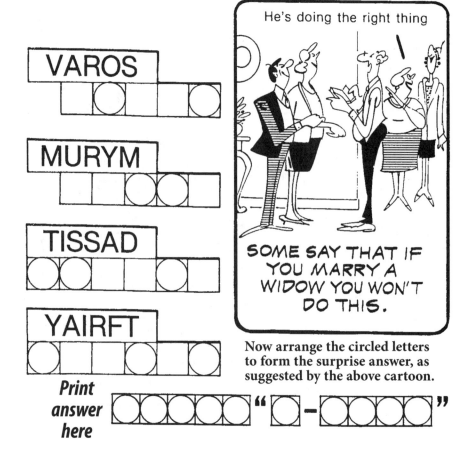

He's doing the right thing

SOME SAY THAT IF YOU MARRY A WIDOW YOU WON'T DO THIS.

Now arrange the circled letters to form the surprise answer, as suggested by the above cartoon.

Print answer here

□□□□□ " □ - □□□□ "

JUMBLE®

Unscramble these four Jumbles, one letter to each square, to form four ordinary words.

CRAFS

LIPUP

ENJUKT

BUSUDE

WHAT TEACHER DID WHEN THE ANTELOPE TOOK HIS FINAL EXAM.

Now arrange the circled letters to form the surprise answer, as suggested by the above cartoon.

Print answer here ⬡⬡⬡⬡⬡⬡ THE ⬡⬡⬡⬡

JUMBLE®

Unscramble these four Jumbles, one letter to each square, to form four ordinary words.

YEMON

RUPOC

CRUVSY

TREMIC

It's gen-u-wine

WHAT THE SWINDLER'S POSTURE WAS.

Now arrange the circled letters to form the surprise answer, as suggested by the above cartoon.

Print answer here " ◯◯◯◯◯◯◯◯◯◯ "

JUMBLE®

Unscramble these four Jumbles, one letter
to each square, to form four ordinary words.

NICEW

CUMSI

YATIRR

DROINO

A POLITICIAN IS A
MAN WHO'S SWORN IN-
TO OFFICE AND THEN
THIS AFTERWARDS.

Now arrange the circled letters
to form the surprise answer, as
suggested by the above cartoon.

Print answer here

JUMBLE®

Unscramble these four Jumbles, one letter
to each square, to form four ordinary words.

YATHS

RICHA

LUMUTT

DOSTIL

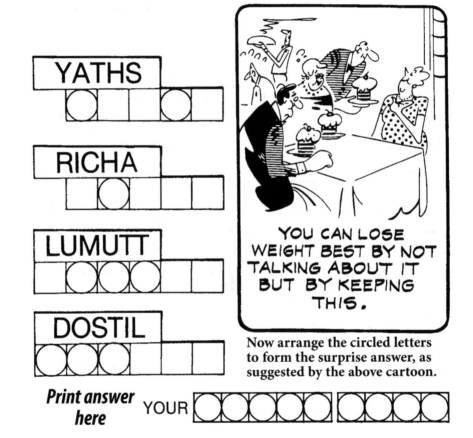

YOU CAN LOSE WEIGHT BEST BY NOT TALKING ABOUT IT BUT BY KEEPING THIS.

Now arrange the circled letters
to form the surprise answer, as
suggested by the above cartoon.

Print answer here   YOUR ☐☐☐☐☐ ☐☐☐☐

JUMBLE®

Unscramble these four Jumbles, one letter
to each square, to form four ordinary words.

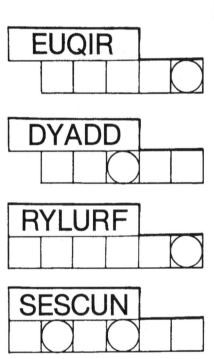

EUQIR

DYADD

RYLURF

SESCUN

A YOUNG MAN WHO
SPENDS TOO MUCH
TIME SOWING HIS
WILD OATS MIGHT
BEGIN TO LOOK THIS.

Now arrange the circled letters
to form the surprise answer, as
suggested by the above cartoon.

Print answer here " ◯◯◯◯◯ "

JUMBLE®

Unscramble these four Jumbles, one letter
to each square, to form four ordinary words.

LOOFI

RATIE

TUVIRE

WYLLOH

Now arrange the circled letters
to form the surprise answer, as
suggested by the above cartoon.

*Print answer
here*

JUMBLE®

Unscramble these four Jumbles, one letter
to each square, to form four ordinary words.

SELLI

AGDEA

BRAJEB

DOBOLY

Lots of men
of vision here

And
women,
too

WHAT THE
OPHTHALMOLOGISTS
CALLED THEIR
ANNUAL SHINDIG.

Now arrange the circled letters
to form the surprise answer, as
suggested by the above cartoon.

Print answer here THE " ◯◯◯ ◯◯◯◯ "

JUMBLE®

Unscramble these four Jumbles, one letter
to each square, to form four ordinary words.

KELLN

GYKAW

MORLAN

BEATED

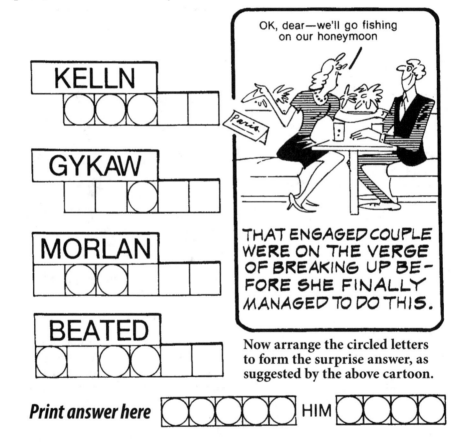

OK, dear—we'll go fishing
on our honeymoon

THAT ENGAGED COUPLE
WERE ON THE VERGE
OF BREAKING UP BE-
FORE SHE FINALLY
MANAGED TO DO THIS.

Now arrange the circled letters
to form the surprise answer, as
suggested by the above cartoon.

Print answer here ⎕⎕⎕⎕⎕ HIM ⎕⎕⎕⎕

JUMBLE®

Unscramble these four Jumbles, one letter to each square, to form four ordinary words.

RONOC

NORST

DIMRAY

CHROID

If she'll only say "yes"

WHAT A MAN SOMETIMES GETS FROM A WOMAN WHO LOOKS LIKE A DREAM.

Now arrange the circled letters to form the surprise answer, as suggested by the above cartoon.

Print answer here

JUMBLE®

Unscramble these four Jumbles, one letter to each square, to form four ordinary words.

DULGI

ROAHB

THINGK

KNEBOC

I like a man who tells it to me straight

BACK TALK IS OFTEN MORE HONEST THAN THIS KIND OF TALK.

Now arrange the circled letters to form the surprise answer, as suggested by the above cartoon.

Print answer here ⬡⬡⬡⬡⬡⬡ - THE - ⬡⬡⬡⬡

JUMBLE®

Unscramble these four Jumbles, one letter
to each square, to form four ordinary words.

DRAIP

EMAHR

GLYNIK

CONTOY

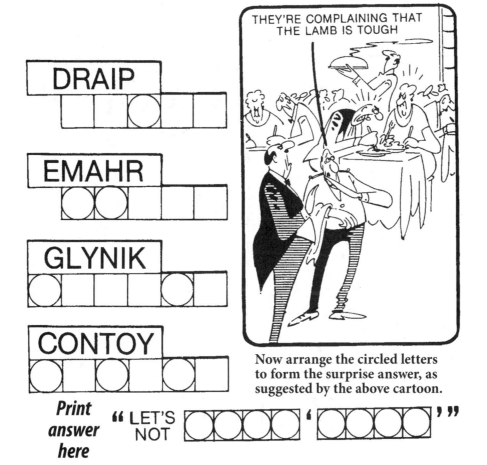

THEY'RE COMPLAINING THAT
THE LAMB IS TOUGH

Now arrange the circled letters
to form the surprise answer, as
suggested by the above cartoon.

Print
answer
here

" LET'S
NOT ' '"

JUMBLE®

Unscramble these four Jumbles, one letter
to each square, to form four ordinary words.

YOLID

VREEV

TARYEW

NARXLY

She'd better
watch her step

WHEN A WOMAN
"FISHES" FOR A
HUSBAND SHE
SHOULD KNOW THIS.

Now arrange the circled letters
to form the surprise answer, as
suggested by the above cartoon.

*Print
answer
here*

WHERE ⬡⬡⬡⬡⬡⬡ THE ⬡⬡⬡⬡

JUMBLE®
Jubilation

Daily
Puzzles

JUMBLE®

Unscramble these four Jumbles, one letter
to each square, to form four ordinary words.

SETAC

FLABE

YEASUN

REPTIL

HOW THAT
ORCHESTRA PLAYER
KEPT HIS TEETH
IN SHAPE.

Now arrange the circled letters
to form the surprise answer, as
suggested by the above cartoon.

Print
answer
here

WITH " " "

JUMBLE®

Unscramble these four Jumbles, one letter to each square, to form four ordinary words.

ENCIE

UNDEC

CATLEK

REVEWS

Going nowhere in his career

A GUY WHO WORKS AT THIS DOESN'T HAVE MUCH CHANCE OF GETTING AHEAD.

Now arrange the circled letters to form the surprise answer, as suggested by the above cartoon.

Print answer here

JUMBLE®

Unscramble these four Jumbles, one letter
to each square, to form four ordinary words.

GUBEN

DAJED

REWESK

LINCEY

They say he's got a
bundle put away

WHAT A GREEN
THUMB CAN MEAN
FOR A PROFESSIONAL
GARDENER.

Now arrange the circled letters
to form the surprise answer, as
suggested by the above cartoon.

**Print answer
here** "   "

JUMBLE®

Unscramble these four Jumbles, one letter
to each square, to form four ordinary words.

VUCER

HERBT

ZEEMYN

RAWHOR

WHAT THE MALE
SHEEP SHOUTED IN
ORDER TO GET HIS
MATE'S ATTENTION.

Now arrange the circled letters
to form the surprise answer, as
suggested by the above cartoon.

Print answer here " ☐☐☐ , ☐☐☐ "

JUMBLE®

Unscramble these four Jumbles, one letter
to each square, to form four ordinary words.

YUSHK

COAME

FLYJOU

THELAH

WHEN A COWARD
GETS INTO A "JAM,"
YOU CAN EXPECT
HIM TO DO THIS.

Now arrange the circled letters
to form the surprise answer, as
suggested by the above cartoon.

**Print
answer
here**

⬡⬡⬡⬡⬡ LIKE ⬡⬡⬡⬡⬡

JUMBLE®

Unscramble these four Jumbles, one letter to each square, to form four ordinary words.

TISOF

PHAMC

SLYGUN

CYMTIS

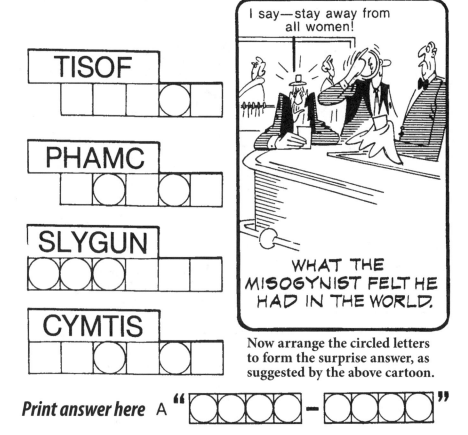

I say—stay away from all women!

WHAT THE MISOGYNIST FELT HE HAD IN THE WORLD.

Now arrange the circled letters to form the surprise answer, as suggested by the above cartoon.

Print answer here A "◯◯◯◯◯ – ◯◯◯◯◯"

JUMBLE®

Unscramble these four Jumbles, one letter
to each square, to form four ordinary words.

HASAB

YAHNE

VISWEL

KADMAS

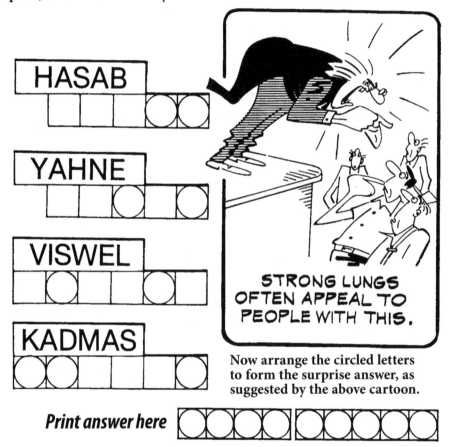

STRONG LUNGS
OFTEN APPEAL TO
PEOPLE WITH THIS.

Now arrange the circled letters
to form the surprise answer, as
suggested by the above cartoon.

Print answer here

JUMBLE®

Unscramble these four Jumbles, one letter to each square, to form four ordinary words.

BAYBE

KECHO

LOVEUM

GETURT

Won't be long before we look like them

AGE MAY BE THE DIFFERENCE BETWEEN THESE.

Now arrange the circled letters to form the surprise answer, as suggested by the above cartoon.

Print answer here

A ◯◯◯◯◯ & A ◯◯◯◯◯

JUMBLE®

Unscramble these four Jumbles, one letter to each square, to form four ordinary words.

RAMER

MEERY

HOBLED

GOTSDY

It's about time you got some new ones

A COMFORTABLE OLD SHOE MIGHT BE THIS, THROUGH THICK AND THIN.

Now arrange the circled letters to form the surprise answer, as suggested by the above cartoon.

Print answer here   YOUR "⬡⬡⬡⬡⬡" ⬡⬡⬡⬡

JUMBLE®

Unscramble these four Jumbles, one letter to each square, to form four ordinary words.

DAUTI

LEXEP

SCIBEP

DUNOAL

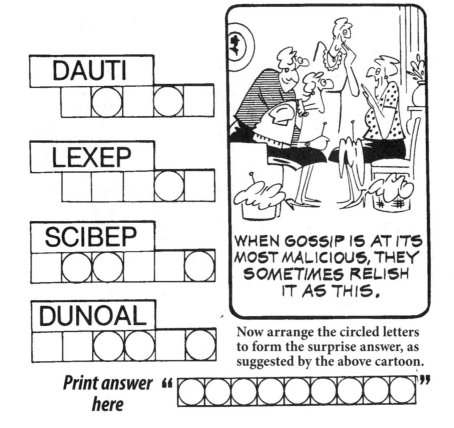

WHEN GOSSIP IS AT ITS MOST MALICIOUS, THEY SOMETIMES RELISH IT AS THIS.

Now arrange the circled letters to form the surprise answer, as suggested by the above cartoon.

Print answer here "◯◯◯◯◯◯◯◯◯◯◯"

JUMBLE®

Unscramble these four Jumbles, one letter
to each square, to form four ordinary words.

CASEE

ROFUL

YARREL

FRINIM

THE CURVE THAT
USUALLY SETS THINGS
STRAIGHT.

Now arrange the circled letters
to form the surprise answer, as
suggested by the above cartoon.

Print answer here

JUMBLE®

Unscramble these four Jumbles, one letter
to each square, to form four ordinary words.

GUSET

SULPH

YURSLE

CIRION

His connections didn't help him

WHAT A CROOKED
POLITICIAN WITH A
"KNOTTY" PROBLEM
MIGHT TRY TO DO.

Now arrange the circled letters
to form the surprise answer, as
suggested by the above cartoon.

*Print answer
here*

JUMBLE®

Unscramble these four Jumbles, one letter to each square, to form four ordinary words.

OATAR

UBLIT

LAMDAY

TIFELL

WORDS OF PRAISE
THAT SELDOM
FALL FLAT.

Now arrange the circled letters to form the surprise answer, as suggested by the above cartoon.

Print answer here

Unscramble these four Jumbles, one letter
to each square, to form four ordinary words.

ERTEX

TEFAC

MOURUQ

PRUINT

We're going to learn how to avoid the mistakes our ancestors made

WHY YOU SHOULD STUDY THE HISTORY OF THE PAST.

Now arrange the circled letters
to form the surprise answer, as
suggested by the above cartoon.

**Print
answer
here** THERE'S A ⭕⭕⭕⭕⭕⭕ ⭕⭕ IT

JUMBLE®

Unscramble these four Jumbles, one letter
to each square, to form four ordinary words.

ALTEM

BUTIC

WHADOS

KRILLE

WHAT HE WOULD DO
EVERY TIME HE SAW
THE GIRL AT THE
CANDY COUNTER.

Now arrange the circled letters
to form the surprise answer, as
suggested by the above cartoon.

Print
answer
here

◯◯◯◯◯ - ◯◯◯◯ HER

JUMBLE®

Unscramble these four Jumbles, one letter to each square, to form four ordinary words.

FLECT

REBBI

LIFEED

TACTIN

He's writing to himself

THE EGOTIST'S LOVE LETTER.

Now arrange the circled letters to form the surprise answer, as suggested by the above cartoon.

Print answer here THE ⬭⬭⬭⬭⬭⬭ "⬭"

JUMBLE®

Unscramble these four Jumbles, one letter to each square, to form four ordinary words.

INGOR

DERIN

REECCO

SAFTIE

WHEN THE SKUNK ENTERED THE ROOM IT GOT ATTENTION BE-CAUSE IT WAS THIS.

Now arrange the circled letters to form the surprise answer, as suggested by the above cartoon.

Print answer here THE " ⬡⬡⬡⬡⬡⬡⬡ " OF IT

JUMBLE®

Unscramble these four Jumbles, one letter
to each square, to form four ordinary words.

MOWNE

NASPY

REOCAN

CREBIK

Must be the
weather

TEMPORARILY
CLOSED

WHERE THE DEPOSITS
ARE "FROZEN ASSETS."

Now arrange the circled letters
to form the surprise answer, as
suggested by the above cartoon.

Print answer here   IN A " ◯◯◯◯ ◯◯◯◯ "

JUMBLE®

Unscramble these four Jumbles, one letter
to each square, to form four ordinary words.

LEETA

NUMIS

SLEPEN

MUDINS

Expect me to wait all day?

THE NERVOUS TAILOR
WAS ALWAYS
ON THIS.

Now arrange the circled letters
to form the surprise answer, as
suggested by the above cartoon.

Print answer here ◯◯◯◯◯ & ◯◯◯◯◯◯◯◯◯

JUMBLE®

Unscramble these four Jumbles, one letter
to each square, to form four ordinary words.

YOVIR

RODIF

THANYS

CAFEED

THAT WELL-DRESSED
WOMAN WAS INDEED A
CREDIT TO HER HUS-
BAND, THANKS TO THIS.

Now arrange the circled letters
to form the surprise answer, as
suggested by the above cartoon.

Print answer here

JUMBLE®

Unscramble these four Jumbles, one letter
to each square, to form four ordinary words.

AVERB

RESEA

DAUPIN

YUCLOD

WHEN YOU CALL THE
PLUMBER BECAUSE OF
A LEAK IT MIGHT
END UP BEING THIS.

Now arrange the circled letters
to form the surprise answer, as
suggested by the above cartoon.

Print answer
here

A " ☐☐☐☐☐☐ " ON ☐☐☐

JUMBLE®

Unscramble these four Jumbles, one letter to each square, to form four ordinary words.

YENED

BROAN

DEECES

SLETED

How beautiful

I wouldn't be too sure

THE JUDGE'S WORDS WERE LESS IMPORTANT THAN THIS.

Now arrange the circled letters to form the surprise answer, as suggested by the above cartoon.

Print answer here HIS ◯◯◯◯◯◯◯◯◯◯◯

JUMBLE®

Unscramble these four Jumbles, one letter
to each square, to form four ordinary words.

He'll go far

VERPO

HEEPS

FUNIES

CIAMAN

WHAT AN EMPLOYEE
HAS IF HE LAUGHS
AT THE BOSS'S JOKES
EVEN WHEN THEY
MAKE NO THIS.

Now arrange the circled letters
to form the surprise answer, as
suggested by the above cartoon.

Print answer here " ◯◯◯◯◯ "

JUMBLE®

Unscramble these four Jumbles, one letter
to each square, to form four ordinary words.

NAKOE

FITAH

CERAPH

PLUCUF

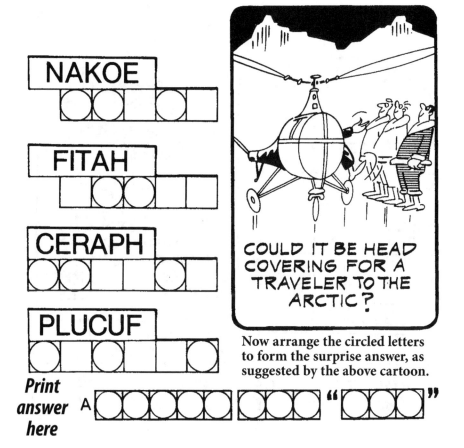

COULD IT BE HEAD
COVERING FOR A
TRAVELER TO THE
ARCTIC?

Now arrange the circled letters
to form the surprise answer, as
suggested by the above cartoon.

Print answer here   A ☐☐☐☐☐☐ ☐☐☐ "☐☐☐"

JUMBLE®

Unscramble these four Jumbles, one letter
to each square, to form four ordinary words.

RIGAN

THICY

MOLDEY

SLAVAS

WHAT HAPPENED WHEN
THEIR SHELLFISH
BUSINESS SUFFERED
FINANCIAL REVERSES?

Now arrange the circled letters
to form the surprise answer, as
suggested by the above cartoon.

**Print answer
here** IT WAS A " ⬡⬡⬡⬡⬡ — ⬡⬡⬡ "

Unscramble these four Jumbles, one letter
to each square, to form four ordinary words.

ULARR

LIVAL

BLUESH

TRAWEY

HE MARRIED A
WOMAN WHO COULD
INDEED TAKE
A JOKE.

Now arrange the circled letters
to form the surprise answer, as
suggested by the above cartoon.

Print answer here ⬡⬡ ⬡⬡⬡ ⬡⬡ !

JUMBLE®

Unscramble these four Jumbles, one letter to each square, to form four ordinary words.

VOYIR

NARCK

DUSSIC

PINKAD

I'm going out with the boys tonight

Oh, no you're not!

SOME MEN DON'T LIKE BEING ORDERED AROUND UNLESS IT'S THIS.

Now arrange the circled letters to form the surprise answer, as suggested by the above cartoon.

Print answer here

A ☐☐☐☐☐ OF ☐☐☐☐☐☐☐

JUMBLE®

Unscramble these four Jumbles, one letter
to each square, to form four ordinary words.

EVASU

HUBOG

GLENET

THROCC

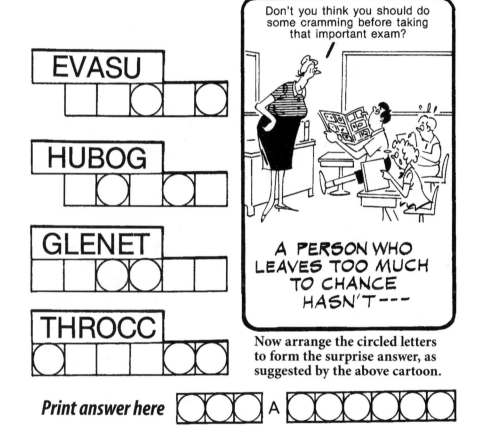

Don't you think you should do
some cramming before taking
that important exam?

A PERSON WHO
LEAVES TOO MUCH
TO CHANCE
HASN'T - - -

Now arrange the circled letters
to form the surprise answer, as
suggested by the above cartoon.

Print answer here ⬡⬡⬡ A ⬡⬡⬡⬡⬡⬡

JUMBLE®

Unscramble these four Jumbles, one letter
to each square, to form four ordinary words.

KIMPS

PLEEX

CATCEN

PENMAD

WHAT THE HOSTS
SAID, WHEN THEIR
WELCOME WAS OUT-
STAYED BY A GUEST.

Now arrange the circled letters
to form the surprise answer, as
suggested by the above cartoon.

Print answer here "  !"

JUMBLE®

Unscramble these four Jumbles, one letter
to each square, to form four ordinary words.

RAMOA

BANIC

GROUME

HATTUG

THAT FORTUNE –
HUNTING BACHELOR
SAID HE WAS NEVER
GOING TO MARRY
UNTIL HE FOUND THIS.

Now arrange the circled letters
to form the surprise answer, as
suggested by the above cartoon.

**Print
answer
here**   THE ⬡⬡⬡⬡⬡ ⬡⬡⬡⬡⬡⬡

JUMBLE®

Unscramble these four Jumbles, one letter to each square, to form four ordinary words.

REBAG

LESIA

NORGAD

PELETS

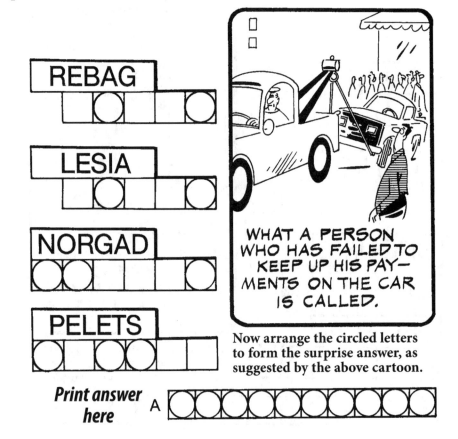

WHAT A PERSON WHO HAS FAILED TO KEEP UP HIS PAYMENTS ON THE CAR IS CALLED.

Now arrange the circled letters to form the surprise answer, as suggested by the above cartoon.

Print answer here A ⬡⬡⬡⬡⬡⬡⬡⬡⬡⬡⬡⬡

JUMBLE®

Unscramble these four Jumbles, one letter
to each square, to form four ordinary words.

VARGE

LIBOR

RICION

DIMFOY

SOMETHING IN A
HAT STORE THAT
MIGHT MAKE YOU
LOOK FOOLISH.

Now arrange the circled letters
to form the surprise answer, as
suggested by the above cartoon.

Print answer here A ⟨⟩⟨⟩⟨⟩⟨⟩⟨⟩⟨⟩

JUMBLE®

Unscramble these four Jumbles, one letter
to each square, to form four ordinary words.

DOITI

THERB

PHILSO

BASHUM

Wait'll you hear this...

Wait'll YOU hear THIS!!!

WHEN NEIGHBORS GOSSIP OVER A FENCE, THERE'S MUCH TO BE SAID---

Now arrange the circled letters
to form the surprise answer, as
suggested by the above cartoon.

Print answer here ON ☐☐☐☐ ☐☐☐☐☐

JUMBLE®

Unscramble these four Jumbles, one letter
to each square, to form four ordinary words.

MILPE

LYDIO

REYJES

DINNAL

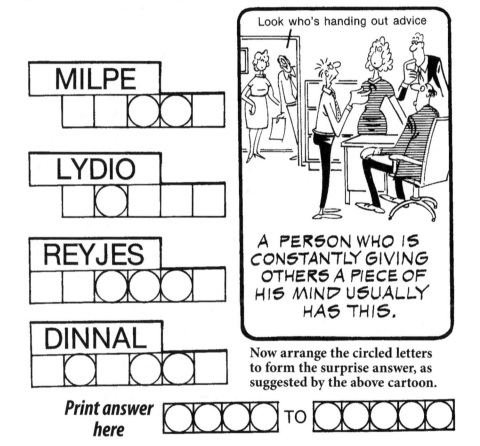

Look who's handing out advice

A PERSON WHO IS
CONSTANTLY GIVING
OTHERS A PIECE OF
HIS MIND USUALLY
HAS THIS.

Now arrange the circled letters
to form the surprise answer, as
suggested by the above cartoon.

**Print answer
here** ☐☐☐☐☐ TO ☐☐☐☐☐☐

JUMBLE®

Unscramble these four Jumbles, one letter to each square, to form four ordinary words.

WOGIN

YOOTS

PROTTE

ENBRAY

Today's project--law enforcement

A SINGLE WORD THAT MAY TAKE THE PLACE OF A LONG SENTENCE.

Now arrange the circled letters to form the surprise answer, as suggested by the above cartoon.

Print answer here " ◯◯◯◯◯◯◯◯◯◯ "

JUMBLE®

Unscramble these four Jumbles, one letter to each square, to form four ordinary words.

NARFC

DALLE

LIMSAD

INCLEY

Then it's settled--I own 'em all!

THE EGOCENTRIC IS SELDOM CON-CERNED WITH IDEALS, BUT ALWAYS WITH ---

Now arrange the circled letters to form the surprise answer, as suggested by the above cartoon.

Print answer here " ☐ " ☐☐☐☐☐

JUMBLE

Unscramble these four Jumbles, one letter
to each square, to form four ordinary words.

TOCET

ATEAB

POMLEY

INPURT

I'll take care of you later

WHAT A
SUCCESSFUL HEAD-
WAITER IS.

Now arrange the circled letters
to form the surprise answer, as
suggested by the above cartoon.

Print answer here " ◯◯◯ – ◯◯◯ "

JUMBLE®

Unscramble these four Jumbles, one letter
to each square, to form four ordinary words.

BAFLE

SOSAB

TENSOL

DRENGE

WHAT THAT
ELOQUENT CRIMINAL
LAWYER USED ON
THE JURY.

Now arrange the circled letters
to form the surprise answer, as
suggested by the above cartoon.

Print answer here " ⬭⬭⬭⬭ ⬭⬭⬭ "

JUMBLE

Unscramble these four Jumbles, one letter
to each square, to form four ordinary words.

PYJUM

DAULT

HATHEL

WURPAD

WHAT THE CHAIR-
MAN OF THE MEETING
DID TO GET SUCH
RAPT ATTENTION.

Now arrange the circled letters
to form the surprise answer, as
suggested by the above cartoon.

Print answer here

JUMBLE®

Unscramble these four Jumbles, one letter
to each square, to form four ordinary words.

NUDAT

CUPAN

SMIBUT

THINEW

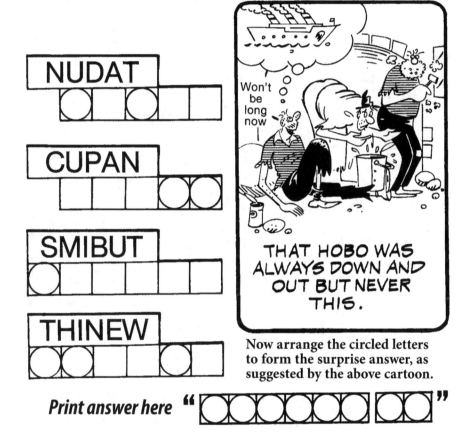

Won't
be
long
now

THAT HOBO WAS
ALWAYS DOWN AND
OUT BUT NEVER
THIS.

Now arrange the circled letters
to form the surprise answer, as
suggested by the above cartoon.

Print answer here " ⬡⬡⬡⬡⬡⬡ ⬡⬡ "

JUMBLE®

Unscramble these four Jumbles, one letter
to each square, to form four ordinary words.

ZUGEA

YILCI

LOOTIN

VINTER

He'll be president
of the company one
of these days

WHAT KIND OF
WIRE MAKES THE
BEST "CONNECTIONS"?

Now arrange the circled letters
to form the surprise answer, as
suggested by the above cartoon.

Print answer here ☐ " ☐☐☐☐ " ☐☐☐

JUMBLE®

Unscramble these four Jumbles, one letter
to each square, to form four ordinary words.

LUFET

EXVIN

UNRATT

CHAPER

As I was saying
YAK YAK YAK YAK

Time
to go,
dear

THE BEST WAY
TO MAKE A LONG
STORY SHORT.

Now arrange the circled letters
to form the surprise answer, as
suggested by the above cartoon.

**Print answer
here** ◯◯◯◯◯◯◯◯◯◯◯ HIM

JUMBLE®

Unscramble these four Jumbles, one letter to each square, to form four ordinary words.

SINUM

LITTE

NEPELS

SHMAIF

WHERE THE PREVARICATOR'S CHARACTER LIES.

Now arrange the circled letters to form the surprise answer, as suggested by the above cartoon.

Print answer here

JUMBLE®

Unscramble these four Jumbles, one letter
to each square, to form four ordinary words.

TIGAN

ABNIS

STUBOE

WOLTAL

OFTEN DRUNK
BUT NEVER
INTOXICATED.

Now arrange the circled letters
to form the surprise answer, as
suggested by the above cartoon.

Print answer here

71

JUMBLE®

Unscramble these four Jumbles, one letter
to each square, to form four ordinary words.

HILEW

POSOW

RELENK

SHOPIN

WHEN THE DENTIST
DOES WORK ON
YOUR TEETH, IT
OFTEN PROVIDES---

Now arrange the circled letters
to form the surprise answer, as
suggested by the above cartoon.

*Print
answer
here*

◯◯◯◯ FOR ◯◯◯ ◯◯◯

JUMBLE®

Unscramble these four Jumbles, one letter
to each square, to form four ordinary words.

ERRAM

DYADD

TEXMEP

MEENAC

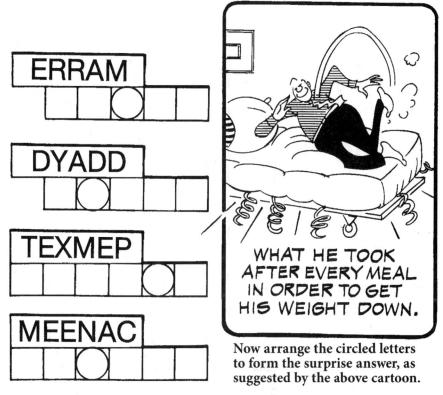

WHAT HE TOOK
AFTER EVERY MEAL
IN ORDER TO GET
HIS WEIGHT DOWN.

Now arrange the circled letters
to form the surprise answer, as
suggested by the above cartoon.

Print answer here

JUMBLE®

Unscramble these four Jumbles, one letter to each square, to form four ordinary words.

YOBOT

SIFIN

TUCSOC

PLESIV

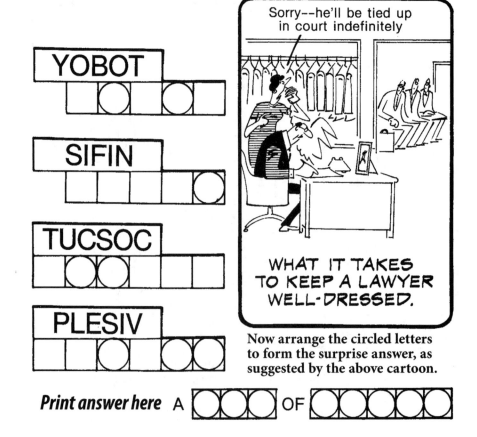

Sorry--he'll be tied up in court indefinitely

WHAT IT TAKES TO KEEP A LAWYER WELL-DRESSED.

Now arrange the circled letters to form the surprise answer, as suggested by the above cartoon.

Print answer here A ⬡⬡⬡ OF ⬡⬡⬡⬡⬡

JUMBLE®

Unscramble these four Jumbles, one letter
to each square, to form four ordinary words.

KALEF

TOORB

SIGUNE

NYWIRT

My, Boss--you look
gorgeous this morning

Really?

A FLATTERER
ALWAYS SAYS THE
RIGHT THING
FOR THIS.

Now arrange the circled letters
to form the surprise answer, as
suggested by the above cartoon.

*Print
answer
here*

THE ◯◯◯◯◯ ◯◯◯◯◯◯

JUMBLE®

Unscramble these four Jumbles, one letter to each square, to form four ordinary words.

TAUDI

PAMCH

RELILK

LAISOC

I never want to see you again--and wash your face

COULD BE THE MARK OF A GREAT LOVER.

Now arrange the circled letters to form the surprise answer, as suggested by the above cartoon.

Print answer here

JUMBLE®

Unscramble these four Jumbles, one letter
to each square, to form four ordinary words.

MOUDI

KANEL

BONGEY

GISTED

Weatherman was
wrong again

HOW SPRING
OFTEN COMES.

Now arrange the circled letters
to form the surprise answer, as
suggested by the above cartoon.

Print answer here " ◯◯◯◯◯◯ – ◯◯ "

JUMBLE®

Unscramble these four Jumbles, one letter to each square, to form four ordinary words.

CREMY

POOTH

SEMQUO

NICKES

He shows more promise now than he did on the "street"

WHERE THE INVESTMENT BANKER TURNED ACTOR COULD REGULARLY BE SEEN.

Now arrange the circled letters to form the surprise answer, as suggested by the above cartoon.

Print answer here IN "_____"

JUMBLE®

Unscramble these four Jumbles, one letter
to each square, to form four ordinary words.

GEELY

ACNIP

UNBOCE

CAFRIB

ANOTHER NAME FOR
ALL THAT BAGGAGE
THAT GOES INTO
THE VEHICLE.

Now arrange the circled letters
to form the surprise answer, as
suggested by the above cartoon.

Print answer here " ⬡⬡⬡ – ⬡⬡ "

JUMBLE®

Unscramble these four Jumbles, one letter
to each square, to form four ordinary words.

MOPET
◯◯□□

DOBOL
□□◯◯□

VARMEL
□□◯◯□◯

PRIMEE
□◯◯◯□

That'll make
the property
nicer

WHAT A SKILLED
GARDENER KNOWS
HOW TO DO.

Now arrange the circled letters
to form the surprise answer, as
suggested by the above cartoon.

**Print
answer
here**   ◯◯◯◯◯◯◯ HIS " ◯◯◯ "

JUMBLE®

Unscramble these four Jumbles, one letter to each square, to form four ordinary words.

We'll take 75% of the gross--every week

IN SOME BUSINESSES IT'S NOT THE OVER-HEAD BUT THIS.

MYLAN

VONEY

SHORUC

IVIDDE

Now arrange the circled letters to form the surprise answer, as suggested by the above cartoon.

Print answer here THE ⬡⬡⬡⬡⬡⬡⬡⬡⬡⬡

JUMBLE®

Unscramble these four Jumbles, one letter to each square, to form four ordinary words.

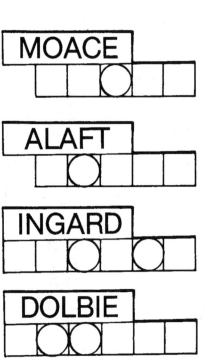

MOACE

ALAFT

INGARD

DOLBIE

You're grounded!

WHAT A PARENT'S MAJOR PROBLEM SOMETIMES IS.

Now arrange the circled letters to form the surprise answer, as suggested by the above cartoon.

Print answer here

JUMBLE®

Unscramble these four Jumbles, one letter to each square, to form four ordinary words.

VARBE

THILE

DAWMOE

LUPPER

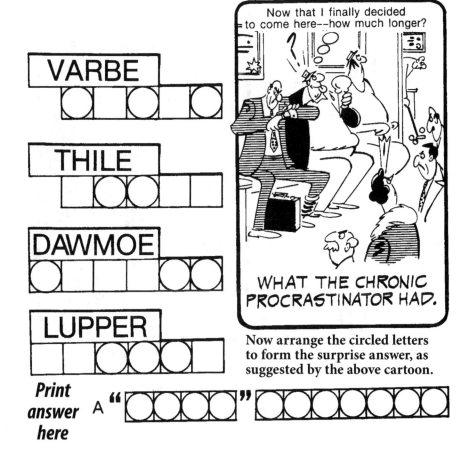

Now that I finally decided to come here--how much longer?

WHAT THE CHRONIC PROCRASTINATOR HAD.

Now arrange the circled letters to form the surprise answer, as suggested by the above cartoon.

Print answer here

A " ◯◯◯◯ " ◯◯◯◯◯◯◯

JUMBLE®

Unscramble these four Jumbles, one letter
to each square, to form four ordinary words.

USEAT

RYDYL

PLUCUF

LARULP

WHAT THEY CALL A
LOT OF CRUMBS
HELD TOGETHER BY
THEIR OWN DOUGH.

Now arrange the circled letters
to form the surprise answer, as
suggested by the above cartoon.

*Print answer
here* THE ⬡⬡⬡⬡⬡⬡ ⬡⬡⬡⬡⬡

JUMBLE®

Unscramble these four Jumbles, one letter to each square, to form four ordinary words.

CEHOP

FRATE

STANEF

ALCIME

Don't you think you've had enough?

A SELF-INDULGENT GUY NEVER DOES THIS.

Now arrange the circled letters to form the surprise answer, as suggested by the above cartoon.

Print answer here " ◯◯ " ◯◯◯◯◯◯◯

JUMBLE®

Unscramble these four Jumbles, one letter
to each square, to form four ordinary words.

HORAB

CUFOS

ASHRIP

KLAYEC

SHE KNEW HER
HUSBAND LIKE
A BOOK---

Now arrange the circled letters
to form the surprise answer, as
suggested by the above cartoon.

**Print answer
here** A " ◯◯◯◯◯ " ◯◯◯◯

JUMBLE ®

Unscramble these four Jumbles, one letter
to each square, to form four ordinary words.

TREXE

NIRAY

MINDOO

SECCAR

Now arrange the circled letters
to form the surprise answer, as
suggested by the above cartoon.

Print answer here

JUMBLE®

Unscramble these four Jumbles, one letter
to each square, to form four ordinary words.

EDGUF

ALGIE

CLEBUK

NOYRAC

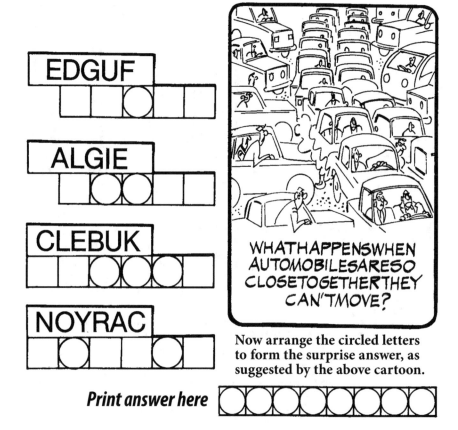

WHATHAPPENSWHEN
AUTOMOBILESARESO
CLOSETOGETHERTHEY
CAN'TMOVE?

Now arrange the circled letters
to form the surprise answer, as
suggested by the above cartoon.

Print answer here

JUMBLE®

Unscramble these four Jumbles, one letter
to each square, to form four ordinary words.

OUDES

MUJOB

DEPENX

CRAFTO

Gorgeous!

WHAT THAT
EXPENSIVE TOUPEE
GOT HIM.

Now arrange the circled letters
to form the surprise answer, as
suggested by the above cartoon.

Print answer here IN ☐☐☐☐☐ OVER HIS ☐☐☐☐☐

89

JUMBLE

Unscramble these four Jumbles, one letter to each square, to form four ordinary words.

SUAPE

DIPTE

RECHIP

UNCANE

The boss's son

Had every advantage

But he'll never get ahead

LOTS OF "PULL" WILL GET YOU ALMOST ANYWHERE, EXCEPT WHEN THIS IS REQUIRED.

Now arrange the circled letters to form the surprise answer, as suggested by the above cartoon.

Print answer here " ◯◯◯◯ "

JUMBLE®

Unscramble these four Jumbles, one letter
to each square, to form four ordinary words.

CUDEN

SAUME

HALLET

TADISS

Now...now...how about you two
having a nice piece of cake

WHAT THOSE
NEIGHBORHOOD BUSY-
BODIES BELONGED TO.

Now arrange the circled letters
to form the surprise answer, as
suggested by the above cartoon.

Print
answer   THE "⬡⬡⬡⬡⬡⬡" ⬡⬡⬡⬡⬡
here

JUMBLE®

Unscramble these four Jumbles, one letter
to each square, to form four ordinary words.

DUBON

POLEE

GLUEED

TRAMOF

WHAT THE
RUG MERCHANT'S
JOKES DID.

Now arrange the circled letters
to form the surprise answer, as
suggested by the above cartoon.

Print answer here ⟨◯◯◯◯◯◯◯⟩ ' ◯◯

JUMBLE®

Unscramble these four Jumbles, one letter to each square, to form four ordinary words.

RONED

GHEED

CHOROB

HOLURY

He pockets plenty

WHAT THE BAKER TURNED COMEDIAN KNEW HOW TO MAKE.

Now arrange the circled letters to form the surprise answer, as suggested by the above cartoon.

Print answer here

◯◯◯◯◯ OUT OF " ◯◯◯◯ "

JUMBLE®

Unscramble these four Jumbles, one letter
to each square, to form four ordinary words.

YEDIT

PARPE

ROVACT

MIDYOF

When is your brother
gonna get a job?

HIS LIFEWORK
WAS TO ---

Now arrange the circled letters
to form the surprise answer, as
suggested by the above cartoon.

Print answer here

JUMBLE®

Unscramble these four Jumbles, one letter to each square, to form four ordinary words.

VOPER

AMLET

FISHTE

SYTHAN

WHAT THEY CALL THAT GUY WHO ALWAYS RE-MAINS AT A PARTY AFTER THE FOOD AND DRINK ARE ALL GONE.

Now arrange the circled letters to form the surprise answer, as suggested by the above cartoon.

Print answer here

JUMBLE®

Unscramble these four Jumbles, one letter
to each square, to form four ordinary words.

MULAB

VAGRE

LARBUT

GLAARN

WHAT THE
BACHELOR'S VIEWS
WERE.

Now arrange the circled letters
to form the surprise answer, as
suggested by the above cartoon.

**Print
answer
here** "◯◯-◯◯◯◯◯-◯◯◯◯"

JUMBLE®

Unscramble these four Jumbles, one letter
to each square, to form four ordinary words.

INGGO

RATAL

ELBARR

WEARLY

Er...if you'll just listen, dear

It's all the boss's fault. He...

WHAT "LITTLE WHITE LIES" USUALLY ARE.

Now arrange the circled letters
to form the surprise answer, as
suggested by the above cartoon.

Print answer here

JUMBLE®

Unscramble these four Jumbles, one letter
to each square, to form four ordinary words.

NACYF

BIMOL

PERUSH

TELKET

Let's appoint a committee

WHAT CONGRESS
PASSED WHEN THEY
COULDN'T THINK OF
ANY NEW LAWS.

Now arrange the circled letters
to form the surprise answer, as
suggested by the above cartoon.

Print answer here ⬡⬡⬡ ⬡⬡⬡⬡⬡

JUMBLE®

Unscramble these four Jumbles, one letter
to each square, to form four ordinary words.

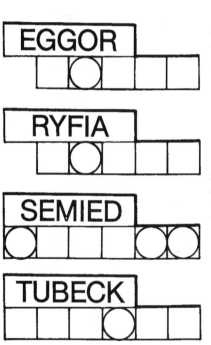

EGGOR

RYFIA

SEMIED

TUBECK

There's a gentleman
waiting to see you

IRS

OFTEN WHEN YOU
SAVE UP FOR A
RAINY DAY YOU END
UP GETTING THIS.

Now arrange the circled letters
to form the surprise answer, as
suggested by the above cartoon.

Print answer here " 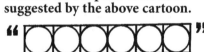 "

JUMBLE®

Unscramble these four Jumbles, one letter
to each square, to form four ordinary words.

INFAL

PRAID

BLOWEB

LAIHNE

This one
gives you
fair value

— No one buys
from him .

WHERE A BUSINESS-
MAN WHO'S ALWAYS
"ON THE LEVEL"
SHOULDN'T HAVE TO GO.

Now arrange the circled letters
to form the surprise answer, as
suggested by the above cartoon.

Print answer here

JUMBLE®

Unscramble these four Jumbles, one letter
to each square, to form four ordinary words.

YEVAH

EUJIC

SEELAW

VISWEL

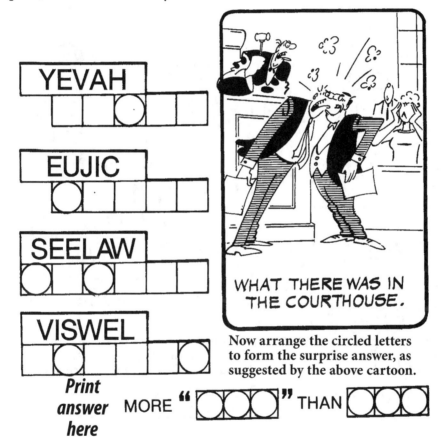

WHAT THERE WAS IN
THE COURTHOUSE.

Now arrange the circled letters
to form the surprise answer, as
suggested by the above cartoon.

Print
answer
here   MORE " ◯◯◯ " THAN ◯◯◯

JUMBLE®

Unscramble these four Jumbles, one letter
to each square, to form four ordinary words.

RIBBE

CLATH

BURPAT

WUNSIE

WHERE THE
SNOBS LIVED.

Now arrange the circled letters
to form the surprise answer, as
suggested by the above cartoon.

Print answer here IN " ◯◯◯◯◯◯◯◯◯ "

JUMBLE®

Unscramble these four Jumbles, one letter
to each square, to form four ordinary words.

DRECY

EVAUM

HASNIB

GOTFER

Uh-oh...I've hurt her
feelings again

WATER POWER THAT
HELPS RUN MANY
HOUSEHOLDS.

Now arrange the circled letters
to form the surprise answer, as
suggested by the above cartoon.

Print answer here

JUMBLE®

Unscramble these four Jumbles, one letter to each square, to form four ordinary words.

GIBEE

VEREF

LOOSCH

CREEFI

THOSE NOISY NEIGH-
BORS THOUGHT THEY
WERE ENJOYING
THE RIGHT OF---

Now arrange the circled letters
to form the surprise answer, as
suggested by the above cartoon.

*Print
answer
here*   " "

JUMBLE®

Unscramble these four Jumbles, one letter
to each square, to form four ordinary words.

THYAS

PEALL

SWEEFT

LIPOCE

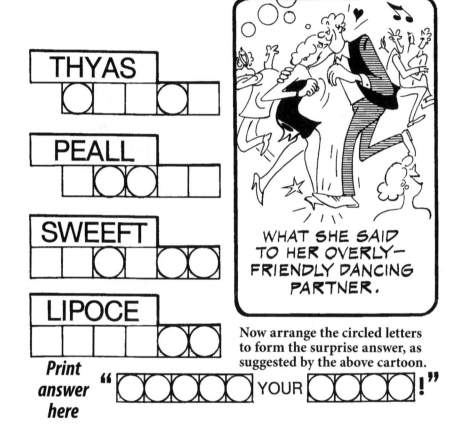

WHAT SHE SAID
TO HER OVERLY—
FRIENDLY DANCING
PARTNER.

Now arrange the circled letters
to form the surprise answer, as
suggested by the above cartoon.

*Print
answer
here*   " ◯◯◯◯◯ YOUR ◯◯◯◯ !"

JUMBLE®

Unscramble these four Jumbles, one letter
to each square, to form four ordinary words.

URFOL

YIPTE

DAYMAL

RERROT

That shack's too small

Need
another
helicopter

HE WASN'T
CONTENTED WITH
HIS LOT—ALWAYS
ASKING FOR THIS.

Now arrange the circled letters
to form the surprise answer, as
suggested by the above cartoon.

Print answer here

JUMBLE®

Unscramble these four Jumbles, one letter
to each square, to form four ordinary words.

VOGEL

KRIHE

INNACE

GOHBUT

WHAT THE NUDIST
CAMP'S STAR
ATHLETE RAN A
HUNDRED YARDS IN.

Now arrange the circled letters
to form the surprise answer, as
suggested by the above cartoon.

Print answer here

JUMBLE®

Unscramble these four Jumbles, one letter
to each square, to form four ordinary words.

KREAM

GUCHO

BLITAR

WHARRO

AS SHE DID THIS,
WORDS PASSED
BETWEEN THEM.

Now arrange the circled letters
to form the surprise answer, as
suggested by the above cartoon.

Print answer
here ⬡⬡⬡⬡⬡ THE ⬡⬡⬡⬡

JUMBLE®

Unscramble these four Jumbles, one letter
to each square, to form four ordinary words.

ENPAC

ILLEB

SELUNS

TROBEH

He earned it every
step of the way

WHOEVER SAID THAT
MONEY GROWS ON
TREES DIDN'T KNOW
THAT YOU'VE
ALSO GOT TO ---

Now arrange the circled letters
to form the surprise answer, as
suggested by the above cartoon.

Print
answer
here

⬡⬡⬡⬡ THE ⬡⬡⬡⬡⬡⬡ FOR
IT

JUMBLE®

Unscramble these four Jumbles, one letter
to each square, to form four ordinary words.

MARRO

ALCAN

NAITOR

HANCUL

HOW MOST THINGS
ARE SOLD IN A
SUPERMARKET.

Now arrange the circled letters
to form the surprise answer, as
suggested by the above cartoon.

☐☐☐☐ " ☐☐☐☐☐ "

JUMBLE®

Unscramble these four Jumbles, one letter to each square, to form four ordinary words.

SNOBI

LERIN

CAJEKT

IPCINC

WHAT'S THE ONLY ILLNESS YOU CAN CATCH FROM A HYPOCHONDRIAC?

Now arrange the circled letters to form the surprise answer, as suggested by the above cartoon.

Print answer here   A ⟨⟩⟨⟩⟨⟩⟨⟩ IN THE ⟨⟩⟨⟩⟨⟩⟨⟩

JUMBLE®

Unscramble these four Jumbles, one letter to each square, to form four ordinary words.

POSOT
◯◯◯◯

LAQUI
◯◯◯

ENGOIP
◯◯◯◯◯

PHORGE
◯◯◯◯

What's the latest gossip, Mr. Schultz?

HOW TO FIND OUT WHAT'S UP.

Now arrange the circled letters to form the surprise answer, as suggested by the above cartoon.

Print answer here ◯◯ ◯◯◯◯◯◯◯◯

JUMBLE®

Unscramble these four Jumbles, one letter to each square, to form four ordinary words.

NOONI

SPTYI

TARPYN

NILMEG

Those are amazing!

Wow! You really came through.

Aidan's Arrangements

WHEN CHALLENGED TO DELIVER SUCH A HUGE BOUQUET FOR THE SPECIAL OCCASION, THE FLORIST ---

Now arrange the circled letters to form the surprise answer, as suggested by the above cartoon.

Print answer here

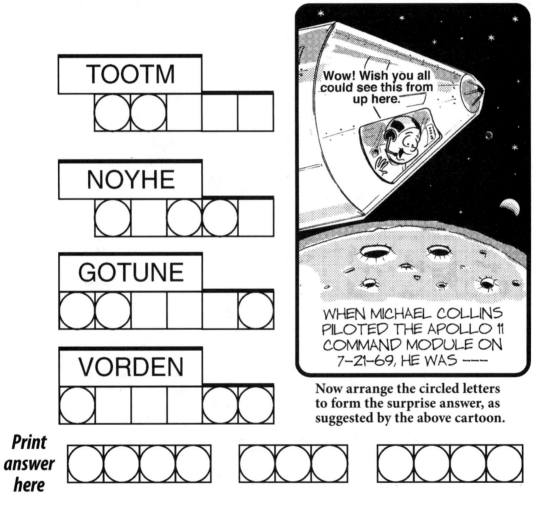

JUMBLE

Unscramble these four Jumbles, one letter
to each square, to form four ordinary words.

TOOTM

NOYHE

GOTUNE

VORDEN

Wow! Wish you all
could see this from
up here.

WHEN MICHAEL COLLINS
PILOTED THE APOLLO 11
COMMAND MODULE ON
7-21-69, HE WAS ----

Now arrange the circled letters
to form the surprise answer, as
suggested by the above cartoon.

Print
answer
here

JUMBLE®

Unscramble these four Jumbles, one letter
to each square, to form four ordinary words.

UGEND

VEPOR

DOINIE

CORLLS

So, if you see two shields and
a boat, it means, "invade".

Why
don't we
just blow
the horn?

WHEN THE VIKING LEADER
NEEDED A NEW MEANS
OF COMMUNICATION,
HE INVENTED ----

Now arrange the circled letters
to form the surprise answer, as
suggested by the above cartoon.

Print answer
here " ⬡⬡⬡⬡⬡ " ⬡⬡⬡⬡

JUMBLE®

Unscramble these four Jumbles, one letter
to each square, to form four ordinary words.

FUTNI

WOLAL

CEDSEE

TTHGIS

Only a master
balloon artist, like
myself, can make
unicorns.

I'd like to burst
his balloon.

Wow!

CASSIDY'S
BALLOON
CREATIONS

WHEN IT CAME TO MAKING
BALLOON ANIMALS,
THIS GUY HAD AN ---

Now arrange the circled letters
to form the surprise answer, as
suggested by the above cartoon.

**Print
answer
here**

JUMBLE®

Unscramble these four Jumbles, one letter
to each square, to form four ordinary words.

NIHYS

DITGI

KNEWAA

GORUCA

Here, we have Bugs.
He likes his carrots.

What's
up,
Doc?

I bet
we'll be
buddies.

Meep!
Meep!

DAFFY DUCK WAS RETIRING
AND HE TOOK THE DUCK
REPLACING HIM ----

Now arrange the circled letters
to form the surprise answer, as
suggested by the above cartoon.

Print
answer
here

JUMBLE®

Unscramble these four Jumbles, one letter to each square, to form four ordinary words.

XEYOP

PILME

TYREKU

ASACUB

No. We need Model Master glue. It's the best!

Best Bond is on sale. It will work fine for you.

Best Bond

WHEN IT CAME TO BUYING THE RIGHT GLUE FOR THEIR MODEL AIRPLANE, HIS FATHER WAS BEING A ----

Now arrange the circled letters to form the surprise answer, as suggested by the above cartoon.

Print answer here

JUMBLE®

Unscramble these four Jumbles, one letter to each square, to form four ordinary words.

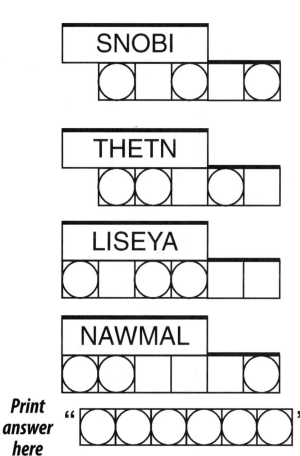

SNOBI

THETN

LISEYA

NAWMAL

I play the winner.

THE PING-PONG PLAYING HORSES WERE ENJOYING THEIR GAME OF ----

Now arrange the circled letters to form the surprise answer, as suggested by the above cartoon.

Print answer here

" ◯◯◯◯◯◯ " ◯◯◯◯◯◯

JUMBLE®

Unscramble these four Jumbles, one letter to each square, to form four ordinary words.

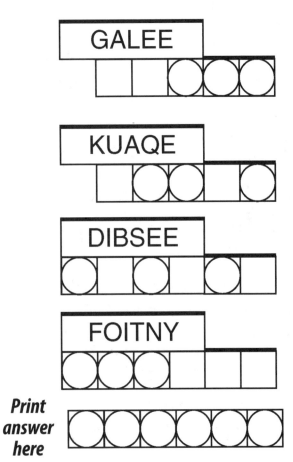

GALEE

KUAQE

DIBSEE

FOITNY

I don't care who is who. You two are in trouble.

We work for you.

What proof do you have?

THE TWINS WHO WORKED FOR THE SPY AGENCY WERE ----

Now arrange the circled letters to form the surprise answer, as suggested by the above cartoon.

Print answer here

JUMBLE®

Unscramble these four Jumbles, one letter to each square, to form four ordinary words.

SILOP

CETJE

COSILA

RONYER

Print answer here

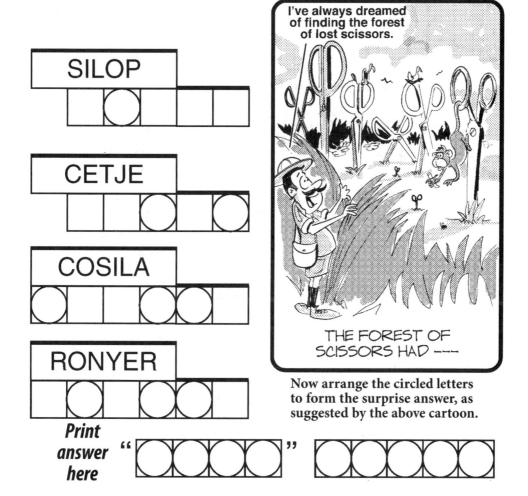

I've always dreamed of finding the forest of lost scissors.

THE FOREST OF SCISSORS HAD ---

Now arrange the circled letters to form the surprise answer, as suggested by the above cartoon.

" ⬡⬡⬡⬡ " ⬡⬡⬡⬡⬡

121

JUMBLE®

Unscramble these four Jumbles, one letter
to each square, to form four ordinary words.

WOLFN

NALTS

KREBAM

GOCCAN

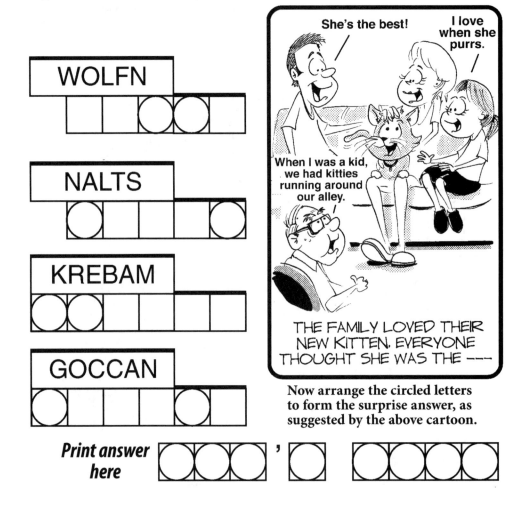

She's the best!

I love when she purrs.

When I was a kid, we had kitties running around our alley.

THE FAMILY LOVED THEIR NEW KITTEN. EVERYONE THOUGHT SHE WAS THE ---

Now arrange the circled letters
to form the surprise answer, as
suggested by the above cartoon.

**Print answer
here**

◯◯◯ ' ◯   ◯◯◯◯◯

JUMBLE®

Unscramble these four Jumbles, one letter to each square, to form four ordinary words.

CPRIH

BULAM

CUPANK

PUEGAL

Thanks for driving. My car's in the shop.

Wow! You look like you could use some coffee.

SHE HAD HER FRIEND DRIVE HER TO THE COFFEE SHOP BECAUSE SHE NEEDED A ---

Now arrange the circled letters to form the surprise answer, as suggested by the above cartoon.

Print answer here

◯◯◯◯ - ◯◯ - ◯◯

JUMBLE®

Unscramble these four Jumbles, one letter
to each square, to form four ordinary words.

VOSHE

FISWT

HILGYH

WAHYON

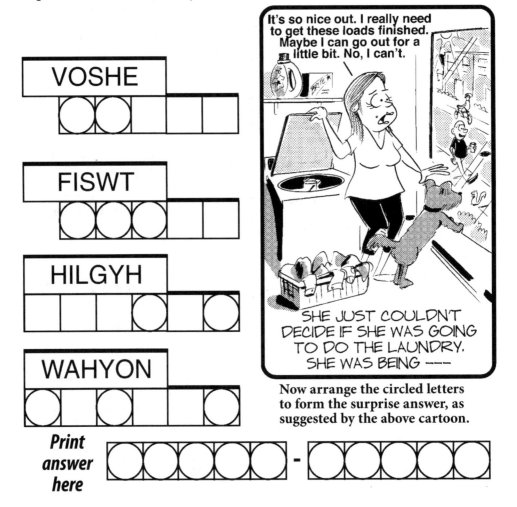

It's so nice out. I really need
to get these loads finished.
Maybe I can go out for a
little bit. No, I can't.

SHE JUST COULDN'T
DECIDE IF SHE WAS GOING
TO DO THE LAUNDRY.
SHE WAS BEING ----

Now arrange the circled letters
to form the surprise answer, as
suggested by the above cartoon.

**Print
answer
here**

◯◯◯◯◯ - ◯◯◯◯◯

JUMBLE®

Unscramble these four Jumbles, one letter to each square, to form four ordinary words.

PALAH

KILYS

LEAGIO

ERREEV

Are you almost finished? You've been at it all day.

I am. I'm exhausted. I need to get some shut-eye.

AFTER CHOPPING FIREWOOD ALL DAY, HE WAS GOING TO ---

Now arrange the circled letters to form the surprise answer, as suggested by the above cartoon.

Print answer here

JUMBLE®

Unscramble these four Jumbles, one letter to each square, to form four ordinary words.

CROLO

OLATT

CHELEK

AMYLUS

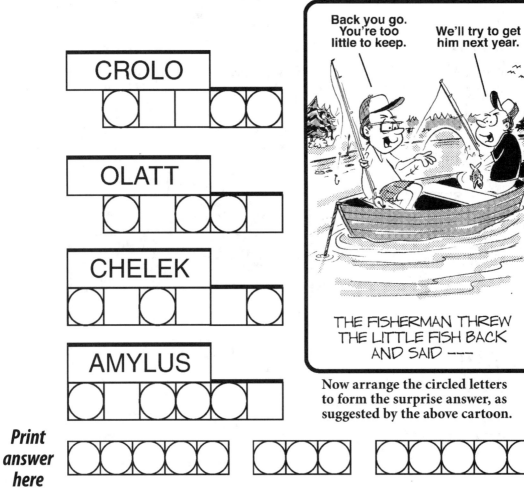

Back you go. You're too little to keep.

We'll try to get him next year.

THE FISHERMAN THREW THE LITTLE FISH BACK AND SAID ---

Now arrange the circled letters to form the surprise answer, as suggested by the above cartoon.

Print answer here

JUMBLE®

Unscramble these four Jumbles, one letter
to each square, to form four ordinary words.

OTARI

BYRED

DOYHDS

HANVEE

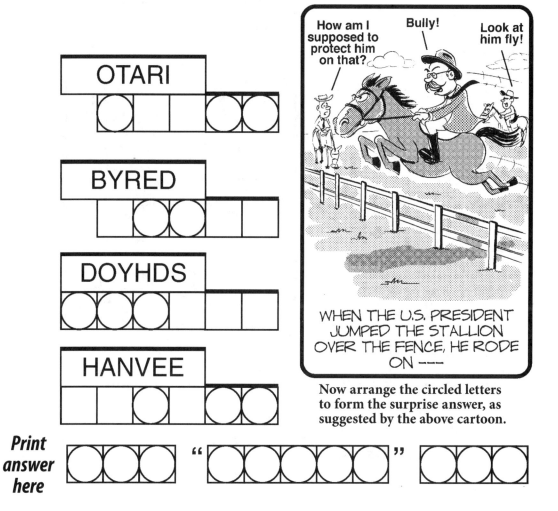

How am I
supposed to
protect him
on that?

Bully!

Look at
him fly!

WHEN THE U.S. PRESIDENT
JUMPED THE STALLION
OVER THE FENCE, HE RODE
ON ----

Now arrange the circled letters
to form the surprise answer, as
suggested by the above cartoon.

*Print
answer
here*

" "

JUMBLE®

Unscramble these four Jumbles, one letter to each square, to form four ordinary words.

LIHEW

DEERL

NAYFIM

MOACTT

Look, there's a bald eagle nest up there.

Up there?

THE PICKPOCKET AT THE BOTTOM OF THE GRAND CANYON WAS A ---

Now arrange the circled letters to form the surprise answer, as suggested by the above cartoon.

Print answer here

JUMBLE®

Unscramble these four Jumbles, one letter to each square, to form four ordinary words.

GANIA

CRODH

MOUSTT

WLIVES

The needle was used to make the grooves. I use the needle to read the grooves and sound comes out of the cone.

That makes sense.

THOMAS EDISON WAS ABLE TO INVENT THE PHONOGRAPH, THANKS TO THE FACT THAT HIS ----

Now arrange the circled letters to form the surprise answer, as suggested by the above cartoon.

Print answer here

JUMBLE®

Unscramble these four Jumbles, one letter
to each square, to form four ordinary words.

VEAUM

ANLAV

BOMENA

MITURA

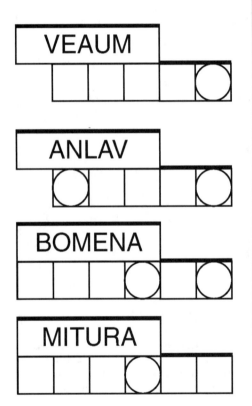

I don't know any
Nigerian Prince! I'm
sick of these scams.

Stop
surfing
and start
walking!

THE TIGHTROPE WALKER
WHO STOPPED TO CHECK
HIS E-MAIL WAS ---

Now arrange the circled letters
to form the surprise answer, as
suggested by the above cartoon.

Print answer here

JUMBLE®

Unscramble these four Jumbles, one letter
to each square, to form four ordinary words.

REQUY

VIOME

SUNSEC

TEANYL

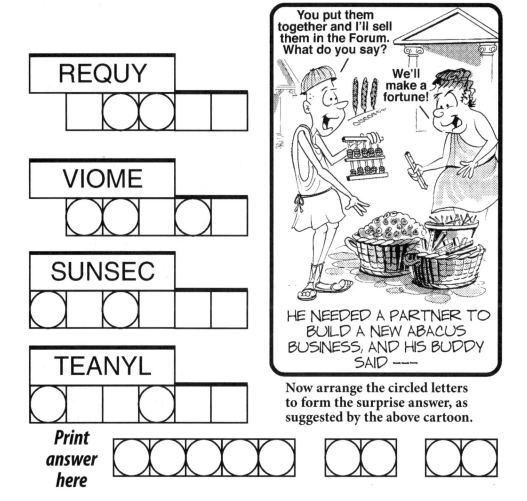

You put them
together and I'll sell
them in the Forum.
What do you say?

We'll
make a
fortune!

HE NEEDED A PARTNER TO
BUILD A NEW ABACUS
BUSINESS, AND HIS BUDDY
SAID ---

Now arrange the circled letters
to form the surprise answer, as
suggested by the above cartoon.

**Print
answer
here**

JUMBLE®

Unscramble these four Jumbles, one letter
to each square, to form four ordinary words.

OGGIN

VROAB

PAWNEO

MEDCYO

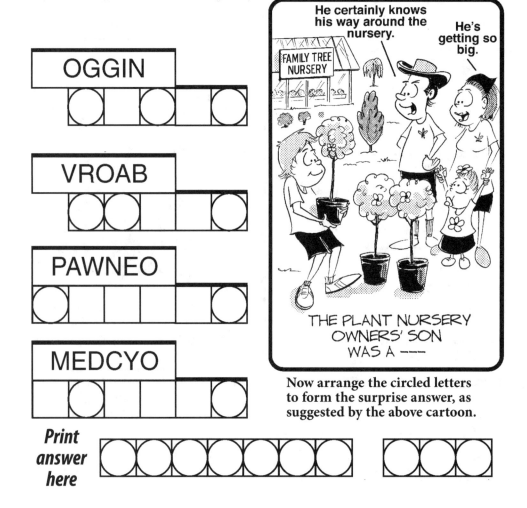

He certainly knows
his way around the
nursery.

He's
getting so
big.

FAMILY TREE
NURSERY

THE PLANT NURSERY
OWNERS' SON
WAS A ---

Now arrange the circled letters
to form the surprise answer, as
suggested by the above cartoon.

Print
answer
here

JUMBLE®

Unscramble these four Jumbles, one letter
to each square, to form four ordinary words.

BURYG

ROCUS

BOCBEW

DAYDEL

That's a
great
idea.

It would also
be a great
place to hide.

WHEN THEY ASKED ROBIN
HOOD IF HE'D LIKE TO HAVE
THEIR NEXT MEETING IN THE
FOREST, HE SAID HE ---

Now arrange the circled letters
to form the surprise answer, as
suggested by the above cartoon.

*Print
answer
here*

JUMBLE®

Unscramble these four Jumbles, one letter to each square, to form four ordinary words.

PERIG

DUNHO

TANTEN

CCINES

He could actually win this if he stays close.

You've got this!

Hurry up!

HE WASN'T FAVORED TO WIN THE MARATHON, BUT HE WAS ----

Now arrange the circled letters to form the surprise answer, as suggested by the above cartoon.

Print answer here

JUMBLE®

Unscramble these four Jumbles, one letter
to each square, to form four ordinary words.

SARBH

SOKIK

NACGEH

LASWUR

You will be taught all the
basics of welding while on
the job as apprentices.

WELDING
101

THE INSTRUCTOR
FOR THE JOB TRAINING
COURSE TAUGHT THE ---

Now arrange the circled letters
to form the surprise answer, as
suggested by the above cartoon.

**Print
answer
here**

JUMBLE®

Unscramble these four Jumbles, one letter
to each square, to form four ordinary words.

TOCEV

WRADN

WRADOC

LAGYLE

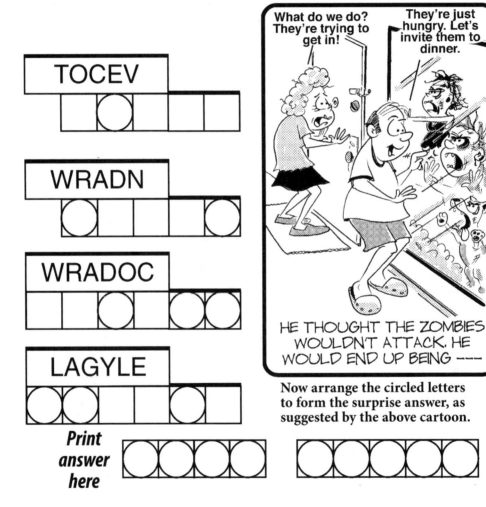

What do we do?
They're trying to
get in!

They're just
hungry. Let's
invite them to
dinner.

HE THOUGHT THE ZOMBIES
WOULDN'T ATTACK. HE
WOULD END UP BEING ---

Now arrange the circled letters
to form the surprise answer, as
suggested by the above cartoon.

Print
answer
here

JUMBLE®

Unscramble these four Jumbles, one letter to each square, to form four ordinary words.

DIRIG

KNITH

GASTIM

PIRMSH

Wow!
I can't believe
how far up we
are.

This is
great!

Why
didn't
we just
float up
here?

WHEN THE GHOSTS
REACHED THE TOP OF
MOUNTAIN, THEY WERE ---

Now arrange the circled letters
to form the surprise answer, as
suggested by the above cartoon.

**Print
answer
here**

JUMBLE®

Unscramble these four Jumbles, one letter
to each square, to form four ordinary words.

CANHO

NATEG

TERXVO

DYLIEE

Aren't you
going to
inspect the
foundation?

I'm sure it's fine.
Everything looks
good from here.

THE TOWER OF PISA'S
BUILDING INSPECTORS
WERE ----

Now arrange the circled letters
to form the surprise answer, as
suggested by the above cartoon.

*Print
answer
here*

" " -

JUMBLE®

Unscramble these four Jumbles, one letter
to each square, to form four ordinary words.

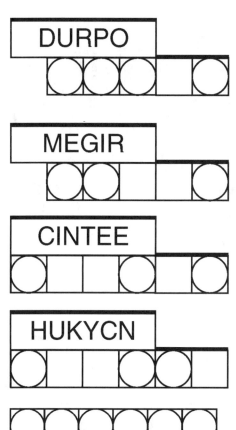

DURPO

MEGIR

CINTEE

HUKYCN

THE USED ALBUM STORE
WOULD EVENTUALLY GO
OUT OF BUSINESS DUE TO
ITS POOR ---

Now arrange the circled letters
to form the surprise answer, as
suggested by the above cartoon.

*Print
answer
here*

JUMBLE®

Unscramble these four Jumbles, one letter
to each square, to form four ordinary words.

INAAV

MALYD

TECERJ

TALEHO

WHEN THE TWINS
PLAYED TENNIS,
THEY WERE ---

Now arrange the circled letters
to form the surprise answer, as
suggested by the above cartoon.

Print
answer
here

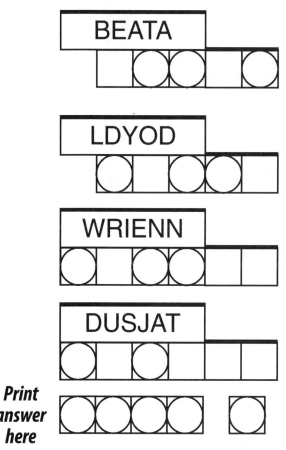

JUMBLE®

Unscramble these four Jumbles, one letter to each square, to form four ordinary words.

BEATA

LDYOD

WRIENN

DUSJAT

Well, that's all for me. I need to find work closer to home.

Good luck.

THE PILOT QUIT BECAUSE HE WANTED TO ---

Now arrange the circled letters to form the surprise answer, as suggested by the above cartoon.

Print answer here

JUMBLE®

Unscramble these four Jumbles, one letter
to each square, to form four ordinary words.

OMYEN

CTART

VORMEE

MAMHEY

How is
she?

She definitely
has a fever.
I'm going to
take her to
the doctor.

WHEN SHE THOUGHT HER
DAUGHTER MIGHT HAVE A
FEVER, SHE USED HER ----

Now arrange the circled letters
to form the surprise answer, as
suggested by the above cartoon.

Print
answer
here

" ⬡⬡⬡⬡⬡ - ⬡⬡⬡ - ⬡⬡⬡⬡⬡ "

JUMBLE®

Unscramble these four Jumbles, one letter to each square, to form four ordinary words.

KIRHE

OBTOR

VINIET

OGATUE

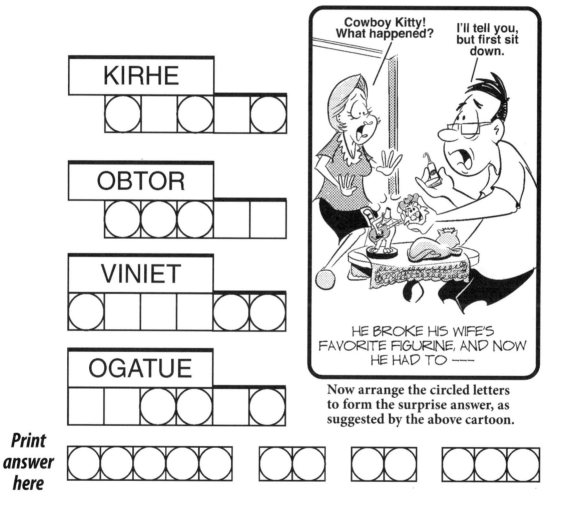

Cowboy Kitty! What happened?

I'll tell you, but first sit down.

HE BROKE HIS WIFE'S FAVORITE FIGURINE, AND NOW HE HAD TO ----

Now arrange the circled letters to form the surprise answer, as suggested by the above cartoon.

Print answer here

JUMBLE®

Unscramble these four Jumbles, one letter
to each square, to form four ordinary words.

KALEY

MYIKL

RANLOM

PUNIRT

Cotton is soft and
strong, but polyester
dries quickly and
wrinkles less.

It doesn't
matter.

$5-Yard

Buy the Yard
Fabrics

THE FABRIC SHE'D
USE TO MAKE A
NEW DRESS WAS ----

Now arrange the circled letters
to form the surprise answer, as
suggested by the above cartoon.

Print
answer
here

JUMBLE®

Unscramble these four Jumbles, one letter
to each square, to form four ordinary words.

VORBA

MILTI

DYIMAD

SENSUL

I need to see
my doctor. I've
had a fever for
a week.

Don't see a doctor.
Just ride it out a
few more weeks.

FOLLOWING HIS FRIEND'S
ADVICE INSTEAD OF SEEING HIS
DOCTOR WAS ----

Now arrange the circled letters
to form the surprise answer, as
suggested by the above cartoon.

Print
answer
here

◯◯◯ - ◯◯◯◯◯◯◯

Unscramble these four Jumbles, one letter
to each square, to form four ordinary words.

ZISEE

CEILR

ULUYNR

UTXODE

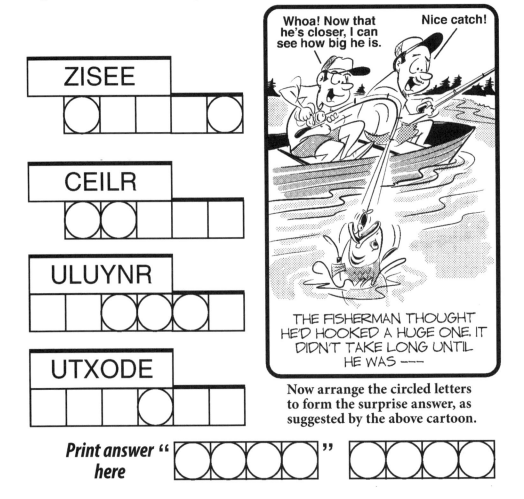

Whoa! Now that
he's closer, I can
see how big he is.

Nice catch!

THE FISHERMAN THOUGHT
HE'D HOOKED A HUGE ONE. IT
DIDN'T TAKE LONG UNTIL
HE WAS ———

Now arrange the circled letters
to form the surprise answer, as
suggested by the above cartoon.

Print answer " ⬡⬡⬡⬡ " ⬡⬡⬡⬡
here

JUMBLE®

Unscramble these four Jumbles, one letter
to each square, to form four ordinary words.

PRAAT

KIKAH

GNUUSF

LEEPTL

Top it off.

Do you want anything?

Want me to check the oil?

GAS-N-GO

COFFEE $1.00

TO REFUEL THE ARMORED
COMBAT VEHICLE,
THEY NEEDED TO ----

Now arrange the circled letters
to form the surprise answer, as
suggested by the above cartoon.

Print answer here

JUMBLE®

Unscramble these four Jumbles, one letter
to each square, to form four ordinary words.

ZDYZI

RHNOO

TIFEDT

GGELIG

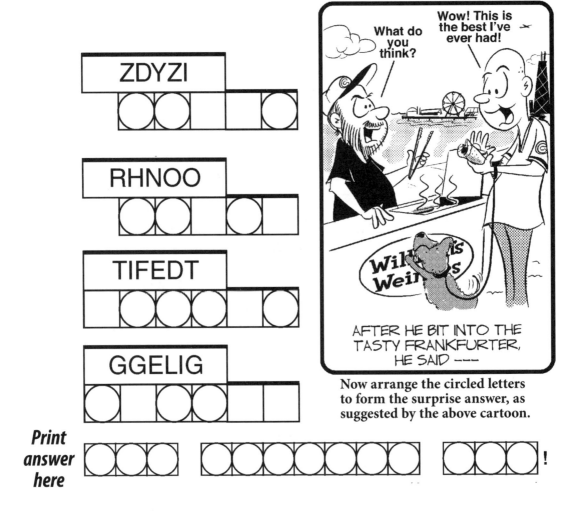

What do
you
think?

Wow! This is
the best I've
ever had!

Wilsons
Weiners

AFTER HE BIT INTO THE
TASTY FRANKFURTER,
HE SAID ---

Now arrange the circled letters
to form the surprise answer, as
suggested by the above cartoon.

*Print
answer
here*
◯◯◯ ◯◯◯◯◯◯◯◯ ◯◯◯!

JUMBLE®

Unscramble these four Jumbles, one letter
to each square, to form four ordinary words.

AUGGE

LAASI

TRONHW

CLASIO

I can't believe my new hammer broke.

My father gave me mine. They don't make them like this anymore.

THE CARPENTER HAS HAD HIS HAMMER FOR SO LONG BECAUSE IT WAS ---

Now arrange the circled letters
to form the surprise answer, as
suggested by the above cartoon.

Print answer here

JUMBLE®

Unscramble these four Jumbles, one letter to each square, to form four ordinary words.

CURKT

MEZAA

NECTAC

EEPPOL

Whoa! I can't believe you survived.

I can't believe that's my sedan!

AFTER GETTING INTO AN ACCIDENT, HER NEW MERCEDES WAS A ---

Now arrange the circled letters to form the surprise answer, as suggested by the above cartoon.

Print answer here

JUMBLE®

Unscramble these four Jumbles, one letter
to each square, to form four ordinary words.

YALBW

FARET

LOBYDL

SEEMSA

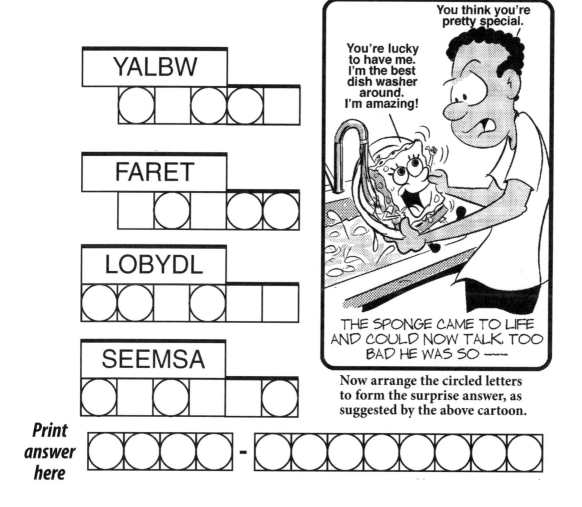

You think you're
pretty special.

You're lucky
to have me.
I'm the best
dish washer
around.
I'm amazing!

THE SPONGE CAME TO LIFE
AND COULD NOW TALK, TOO
BAD HE WAS SO ———

Now arrange the circled letters
to form the surprise answer, as
suggested by the above cartoon.

*Print
answer
here*

◯◯◯◯ - ◯◯◯◯◯◯◯◯◯

JUMBLE®

Unscramble these four Jumbles, one letter
to each square, to form four ordinary words.

DALEG

GEMER

GUNELO

THORYW

THE BRIDE WAS BEAUTIFUL
AND HER HUSBAND-TO-BE
WAS ---

Now arrange the circled letters
to form the surprise answer, as
suggested by the above cartoon.

*Print
answer
here*

◯◯◯◯ - ◯◯◯◯◯◯◯◯

JUMBLE®

Unscramble these four Jumbles, one letter
to each square, to form four ordinary words.

SARHB

WRAND

CTINEE

CHUPCI

We need more help.
Post 15 more
job openings.

TIKI
TIM'S

I'll see what
I can do.
Everyone's
looking for help.

TIKI TIMS
HELP
WANTED

HUMAN RESOURCES

WHEN THE ECONOMY EXPANDS,
THE NUMBER OF NEW JOB
OPENINGS GOES ----

Now arrange the circled letters
to form the surprise answer, as
suggested by the above cartoon.

*Print
answer
here*

" ⎕⎕⎕⎕ " ⎕⎕⎕ " ⎕⎕⎕⎕ "

JUMBLE®

Unscramble these four Jumbles, one letter
to each square, to form four ordinary words.

THFYE

TRUBS

SHIRTT

PARAEP

Hey, slugger! I need
that for your cake
after the game.

Yum! I'll swing
for the fences
today.

WHEN HIS WIFE MADE
CAKE MIX FOR THE BASEBALL
PLAYER, HE SAID ----

Now arrange the circled letters
to form the surprise answer, as
suggested by the above cartoon.

**Print answer
here**

JUMBLE®

Unscramble these four Jumbles, one letter
to each square, to form four ordinary words.

VAHYE

TTUNA

COIZAD

CARDEA

How did this
unflattering
biography of you
get written?

I don't know, but I
want you to write
my new official
biography and I'll
need to approve
every word.

HER OFFICIAL BIOGRAPHY
WOULD BE WRITTEN BY THE
WRITER SHE ---

Now arrange the circled letters
to form the surprise answer, as
suggested by the above cartoon.

*Print
answer
here*

" ◯◯◯◯◯◯ - ◯◯◯◯ "

JUMBLE®

Unscramble these four Jumbles, one letter
to each square, to form four ordinary words.

IFKEN

LONEV

CUROGH

RAVICA

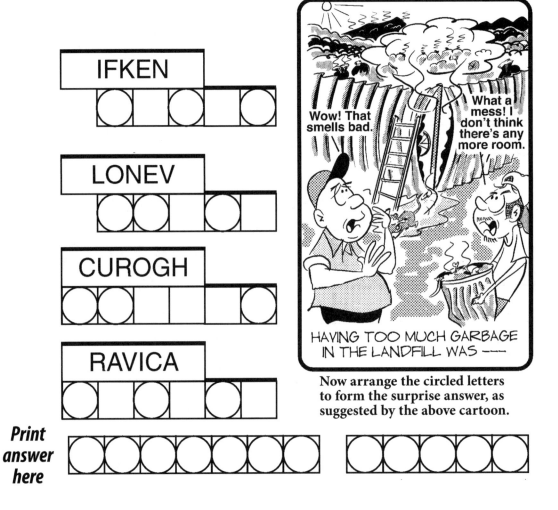

Wow! That smells bad.

What a mess! I don't think there's any more room.

HAVING TOO MUCH GARBAGE
IN THE LANDFILL WAS ---

Now arrange the circled letters
to form the surprise answer, as
suggested by the above cartoon.

**Print
answer
here**

JUMBLE®

Unscramble these four Jumbles, one letter
to each square, to form four ordinary words.

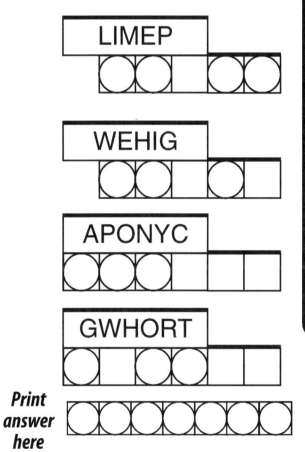

LIMEP

WEHIG

APONYC

GWHORT

What a great,
"Hello." Do you like
your new home?

Looks like
someone
missed us.

WHEN THEY GOT BACK HOME,
THEIR DOGS GREETED THEM
WITH A ----

Now arrange the circled letters
to form the surprise answer, as
suggested by the above cartoon.

**Print
answer
here**

" ❝⃝⃝⃝⃝⃝⃝❞ ,,,

JUMBLE®

Unscramble these four Jumbles, one letter
to each square, to form four ordinary words.

ONINO

NORTF

MAMEHY

DUSBEU

The whole thing
is this small. It
fits right into
my ear.

I didn't know they
could do that.

BEFORE IN-EAR DIGITAL
HEARING AIDS WERE INVENTED,
THEY WERE ----

Now arrange the circled letters
to form the surprise answer, as
suggested by the above cartoon.

**Print
answer
here**

JUMBLE®

Unscramble these four Jumbles, one letter to each square, to form four ordinary words.

SLETY

MIREG

CRIOIN

ARBLER

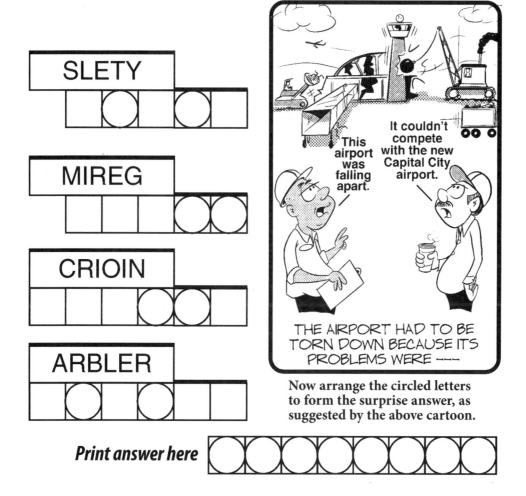

This airport was falling apart.

It couldn't compete with the new Capital City airport.

THE AIRPORT HAD TO BE TORN DOWN BECAUSE ITS PROBLEMS WERE ---

Now arrange the circled letters to form the surprise answer, as suggested by the above cartoon.

Print answer here

JUMBLE®

Unscramble these four Jumbles, one letter to each square, to form four ordinary words.

DOORE

YSLYH

PLOTEP

LITRUA

FAMILY TREE NURSERY

Soon, we'll be sold out.

People just love the way they look between houses.

THE FAST-GROWING TREES WERE SELLING VERY QUICKLY BECAUSE THEY WERE ----

Now arrange the circled letters to form the surprise answer, as suggested by the above cartoon.

Print answer here ◯◯ " ◯◯◯◯◯◯◯ "

JUMBLE®

Unscramble these four Jumbles, one letter to each square, to form four ordinary words.

CULYK

NOEZO

TTINEY

VEINID

Are you ready to head up?

I'd rather take this path.

HOYT HILL ↑
BLUE JAY WAY →

HIS WIFE WANTED TO HIKE UP THE HILL, BUT HE WASN'T ---

Now arrange the circled letters to form the surprise answer, as suggested by the above cartoon.

Print answer here

Unscramble these four Jumbles, one letter
to each square, to form four ordinary words.

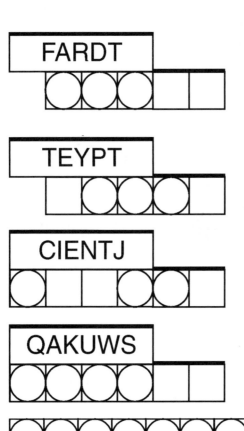

FARDT

TEYPT

CIENTJ

QAKUWS

SHE BOUGHT THE
RESTAURANT,
BUT THE FOOD
WOULD BE AN ---

Now arrange the circled letters
to form the surprise answer, as
suggested by the above cartoon.

*Print
answer
here*

JUMBLE®

Jubilation

Challenger Puzzles

JUMBLE®

Unscramble these six Jumbles, one letter to each square, to form six ordinary words.

HAUTOR

SIMDAL

BELUCK

CLAUNY

FLIDED

MEEGRE

Hard work

THERE WAS NO SKULDUGGERY INVOLVED HERE — JUST THIS.

Now arrange the circled letters to form the surprise answer, as suggested by the above cartoon.

Print answer here

" ⬡⬡⬡⬡⬡ - ⬡⬡⬡⬡⬡⬡⬡⬡ "

JUMBLE®

Unscramble these six Jumbles, one letter to each square, to form six ordinary words.

GRECLY

FOHMAT

JELING

HUMBAS

CANUPH

DANGIR

WHAT YOU MIGHT SEE IN A SEAFOOD RESTAURANT.

Now arrange the circled letters to form the surprise answer, as suggested by the above cartoon.

Print answer here

A " ◯◯◯ ◯◯◯◯◯◯ ◯◯◯◯ "

JUMBLE®

Unscramble these six Jumbles, one letter to each square, to form six ordinary words.

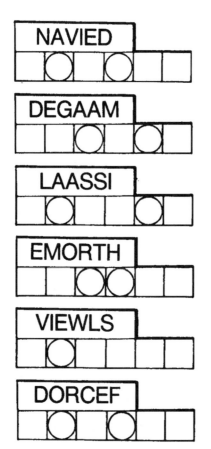

NAVIED

DEGAAM

LAASSI

EMORTH

VIEWLS

DORCEF

I hope you fellows nab those guys!

THE BURGLARS MANAGED TO GET EVERYTHING EXCEPT THIS.

Now arrange the circled letters to form the surprise answer, as suggested by the above cartoon.

Print answer here

◯◯◯◯◯ ' ◯ ◯◯◯◯◯◯◯ TO THEM

JUMBLE®

Unscramble these six Jumbles, one letter
to each square, to form six ordinary words.

YURKET

URBAUN

PEMEXT

PYSEDE

DRAUWP

BRUZZE

WHAT JULIUS CAESAR
PROBABLY KNEW
WHEN HE DEVISED
HIS CALENDAR.

Now arrange the circled letters
to form the surprise answer, as
suggested by the above cartoon.

Print answer here

THAT
HIS ⬭⬭⬭⬭ WERE " ⬭⬭⬭⬭⬭⬭⬭⬭ "

JUMBLE.

Unscramble these six Jumbles, one letter
to each square, to form six ordinary words.

GARAVE

MOUVLE

SOWDRY

LEDENE

TAULOW

HURSTH

HE PRETENDED TO
BE PERFORMING THAT
FAMOUS TRICK, BUT
THE AUDIENCE
FOUND IT THIS.

Now arrange the circled letters
to form the surprise answer, as
suggested by the above cartoon.

Print answer here

TO

JUMBLE®

Unscramble these six Jumbles, one letter
to each square, to form six ordinary words.

TELPOI

BLOORE

THYROW

WETING

MUTTOS

CHOTLE

ELEPHANTS LIVE SO
LONG BECAUSE THEY
NEVER WORRY
ABOUT THIS.

Now arrange the circled letters
to form the surprise answer, as
suggested by the above cartoon.

Print answer here

◯◯◯ TO ◯◯◯◯◯ ◯◯◯◯◯◯◯

JUMBLE®

Unscramble these six Jumbles, one letter to each square, to form six ordinary words.

INREEM

TUFLAR

LANSID

BERROK

GLOBON

SLETED

HOW THE INTRUDER GOT INTO THE HOUSE.

Now arrange the circled letters to form the surprise answer, as suggested by the above cartoon.

Print answer here

" □□ - □□□ - □□□ " □□□□

JUMBLE®

Unscramble these six Jumbles, one letter to each square, to form six ordinary words.

BOIPHS

FRIMAF

RECHOM

GORNTS

NAUMUT

LUDSON

That confirms my research

WHAT THE MEMBERS OF THAT FAMOUS "THINK TANK" USUALLY ENJOYED.

Now arrange the circled letters to form the surprise answer, as suggested by the above cartoon.

Print answer here

" ◯◯◯◯◯ " FOR ◯◯◯◯◯◯◯

171

JUMBLE®

Unscramble these six Jumbles, one letter
to each square, to form six ordinary words.

ALLOCE

HEHRST

HUCCOR

WAYYAN

TIMPER

DURGET

WHY THE SKELETON
WAS AFRAID
TO JUMP OFF.

Now arrange the circled letters
to form the surprise answer, as
suggested by the above cartoon.

Print answer here

172

JUMBLE®

Unscramble these six Jumbles, one letter
to each square, to form six ordinary words.

LATHEC

ELLBOW

TINADY

NAMORT

TAIGEY

YOTHER

WHAT PEOPLE NEED
BEFORE THEY CAN
BUILD A BIG
HOUSE.

Now arrange the circled letters
to form the surprise answer, as
suggested by the above cartoon.

Print answer here

JUMBLE®

Unscramble these six Jumbles, one letter
to each square, to form six ordinary words.

GEDDER

SIRPMH

WAASLY

STIRCP

CONANY

SLIPHO

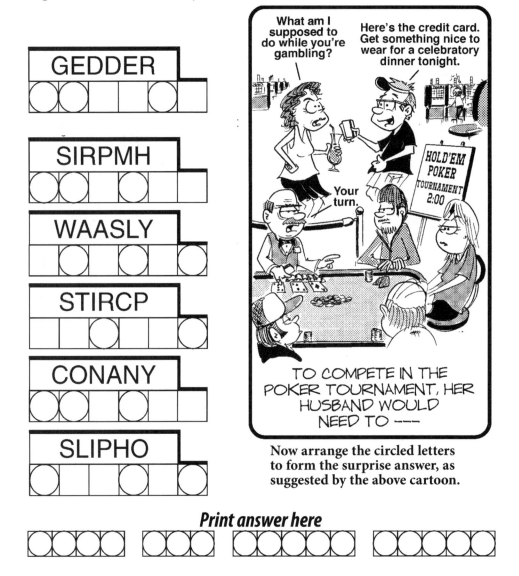

What am I
supposed to
do while you're
gambling?

Here's the credit card.
Get something nice to
wear for a celebratory
dinner tonight.

HOLD'EM
POKER
TOURNAMENT
2:00

Your
turn.

TO COMPETE IN THE
POKER TOURNAMENT, HER
HUSBAND WOULD
NEED TO ----

Now arrange the circled letters
to form the surprise answer, as
suggested by the above cartoon.

Print answer here

JUMBLE®

Unscramble these six Jumbles, one letter to each square, to form six ordinary words.

KNOCLU

GUTBED

SIPEMO

SAUYEN

CENEMA

RIMPRE

Do you like my new toy?

Wow! How many do you own now?

TRSH IT

THANKS TO HIS FLEET OF GARBAGE TRUCKS, THE BUSINESS OWNER HAD ----

Now arrange the circled letters to form the surprise answer, as suggested by the above cartoon.

Print answer here

JUMBLE®

Unscramble these six Jumbles, one letter
to each square, to form six ordinary words.

WYTTEN

REDVON

KORMES

TICNEJ

GREEEM

LIAHEN

We said we'd
be there in
20 minutes.
Can you hurry?

Relax. I'll be finished
when I'm finished.

SUGAR

SHE WAS GOING TO
BRING THE SUGAR
COOKIES WITH HER
SO SHE COULD ----

Now arrange the circled letters
to form the surprise answer, as
suggested by the above cartoon.

Print answer here

Unscramble these six Jumbles, one letter
to each square, to form six ordinary words.

CCROSH

MOSHOC

GAINUA

GLOONB

VOTEMI

LITECI

WITH SO MANY OF HER
CHILDREN THERE,
MOTHER'S DAY WAS A ----

Now arrange the circled letters
to form the surprise answer, as
suggested by the above cartoon.

Print answer here

"◯◯◯ - ◯◯◯◯◯◯" ◯◯◯◯◯◯◯◯

JUMBLE®

Unscramble these six Jumbles, one letter
to each square, to form six ordinary words.

MUREMS

DUTAPE

TAGENE

AILPAM

CABENO

NODFEF

How did they choose
Washington,
Jefferson,
Roosevelt
and Lincoln?

I can't believe
that used to be
a mountain.

WHEN MOUNT RUSHMORE
WAS COMPLETED, PEOPLE
CAME FROM ALL OVER TO
SEE THE ----

Now arrange the circled letters
to form the surprise answer, as
suggested by the above cartoon.

Print answer here

☐☐☐☐☐ " ☐☐☐☐☐ - ☐☐☐☐☐☐ "

JUMBLE®

Unscramble these six Jumbles, one letter to each square, to form six ordinary words.

MIFRON

LOWLOH

MARTEP

GEUNHO

LETHEM

THWICS

This is it! There's no stopping us now. Ready to roll?

Let's go!

Let's start those engines.

HE HADN'T WON THE INDY 500 YET, BUT THE ----

Now arrange the circled letters to form the surprise answer, as suggested by the above cartoon.

Print answer here

JUMBLE®

Unscramble these six Jumbles, one letter to each square, to form six ordinary words.

NUMEMI

DULHED

GHRIFT

TOYPER

BIRBEF

RROLPA

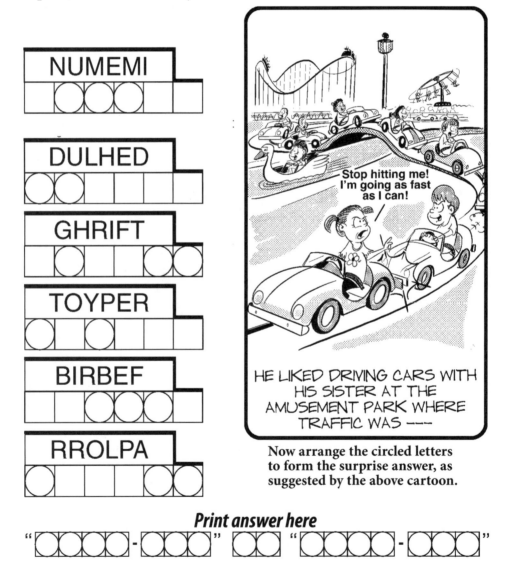

Stop hitting me! I'm going as fast as I can!

HE LIKED DRIVING CARS WITH HIS SISTER AT THE AMUSEMENT PARK WHERE TRAFFIC WAS ----

Now arrange the circled letters to form the surprise answer, as suggested by the above cartoon.

Print answer here

" ⬡⬡⬡⬡-⬡⬡⬡ " ⬡⬡ " ⬡⬡⬡⬡-⬡⬡⬡ "

JUMBLE®

Unscramble these six Jumbles, one letter
to each square, to form six ordinary words.

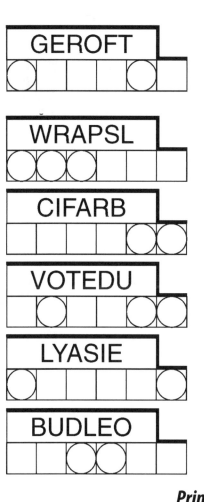

GEROFT

WRAPSL

CIFARB

VOTEDU

LYASIE

BUDLEO

Hopefully, our patrols will keep poachers out.

Farmer Turner is way too lax on security.

Needs more cream.

THE COWS STARTED
PATROLLING THE CATTLE
RANCH AFTER DECIDING THEY
NEEDED TO ----

Now arrange the circled letters
to form the surprise answer, as
suggested by the above cartoon.

Print answer here

JUMBLE®

Unscramble these six Jumbles, one letter to each square, to form six ordinary words.

BAPTEU

CEKNOB

NEEVUA

LEYWOL

PHLULI

STUCAC

No, Harper. Let's let Daddy rest. He looks so peaceful.

THE NEW DAD WAS EXHAUSTED, SO FOR FATHER'S DAY, HIS WIFE LET HIM ----

Now arrange the circled letters to form the surprise answer, as suggested by the above cartoon.

Print answer here

JUMBLE®

Unscramble these six Jumbles, one letter to each square, to form six ordinary words.

NYATIV

PESYEL

POPEOS

NCICIL

RABVLE

CUTLAA

SAN JOSE

I'll set up a website and photoshop some horns on horses.

I finished the email selling unicorn horn powder to cure baldness.

LoL.com

JUMBLE.COM

BIG BELLY

THE FRAUDULENT COMPUTER PROGRAMMERS LIVED IN ---

Now arrange the circled letters to form the surprise answer, as suggested by the above cartoon.

Print answer here

" ◯◯◯◯◯◯ - ◯◯◯◯ " ◯◯◯◯◯◯◯

Answers

1. **Jumbles:** BRAWL EVENT TUSSLE STYMIE
   Answer: With this kind of work, the model never seemed to feel fatigue—"AT-TIRELESS"

2. **Jumbles:** BULGY SKUNK LEEWAY AROUSE
   Answer: What the carpenter who misplaced his tools was—A "SAW" LOSER

3. **Jumbles:** UNITY SAUTE QUENCH CASKET
   Answer: Some people get what they want because they have this—THE "TAKE-NIQUE"

4. **Jumbles:** RUSTY NEWSY BOBBIN POETRY
   Answer: His sandwich arrived squashed because he told the waiter to do this—"STEP ON IT"

5. **Jumbles:** AWASH NUTTY HIDING TIMELY
   Answer: What's the first thing you see after looking for something in the dark?—THE LIGHT

6. **Jumbles:** ENJOY MAXIM GRUBBY MOSQUE
   Answer: What they called that big silent elephant—A "MUM-BO JUMBO"

7. **Jumbles:** POUND GUIDE FONDLY EXCISE
   Answer: What he did when he got that big gas bill—EXPLODED

8. **Jumbles:** HENNA JINGO INDICT POPLIN
   Answer: For him, nothing was so difficult as doing this—NOTHING

9. **Jumbles:** TAWNY VISTA RADIUM POWDER
   Answer: The best way to make a long story short—INTERRUPT

10. **Jumbles:** FLOUT WAGER UNPACK CALICO
    Answer: Ignorance of the law is no excuse, especially if you're this—A KNOW-IT-ALL

11. **Jumbles:** DROOP KETCH CAUCUS ENTICE
    Answer: Some people think that a kid with too much spunk might benefit from a little of this—SPANK

12. **Jumbles:** GUMMY SMACK BEAVER CORRAL
    Answer: The best labor-saving device—A LEGACY

13. **Jumbles:** SAVOR RUMMY SADIST RATIFY
    Answer: Some say that if you marry a widow you won't do this—MARRY "A-MISS"

14. **Jumbles:** SCARF PUPIL JUNKET SUBDUE
    Answer: What the teacher did when the antelope took his final exam—PASSED THE BUCK

15. **Jumbles:** MONEY CROUP SCURVY METRIC
    Answer: What the swindler's posture was—"IMPOSTURE"

16. **Jumbles:** WINCE MUSIC RARITY INDOOR
    Answer: A politician is a man who's sworn into office and then this afterwards—SWORN AT

17. **Jumbles:** HASTY CHAIR TUMULT STOLID
    Answer: You can lose weight best by not talking about it but by keeping this—YOUR MOUTH SHUT

18. **Jumbles:** QUIRE DADDY FLURRY CENSUS
    Answer: A young man who spends too much time sowing his wild oats might begin to look this—"SEEDY"

19. **Jumbles:** FOLIO IRATE VIRTUE WHOLLY
    Answer: A family that lives within its income usually has to learn to do this—LIVE WITHOUT

20. **Jumbles:** LISLE ADAGE JABBER BLOODY
    Answer: What the ophthalmologists called their annual shindig—THE "EYE BALL"

21. **Jumbles:** KNELL GAWKY NORMAL DEBATE
    Answer: That engaged couple were on the verge of breaking up before she finally managed to do this—BREAK HIM DOWN

22. **Jumbles:** CROON SNORT MYRIAD ORCHID
    Answer: What a man sometimes gets from a woman who looks like a dream—INSOMNIA

23. **Jumbles:** GUILD ABHOR KNIGHT BECKON
    Answer: Back talk is often more honest than this kind of talk—BEHIND-THE-BACK

24. **Jumbles:** RAPID HAREM KINGLY TYCOON
    Answer: "They're complaining that the lamb is tough"—"LET'S NOT TALK 'CHOP'"

25. **Jumbles:** DOILY VERVE WATERY LARYNX
    Answer: When a woman "fishes" for a husband she should know this—WHERE TO DRAW THE LINE

26. **Jumbles:** CASTE FABLE UNEASY TRIPLE
    Answer: How the orchestra player kept his teeth in shape—WITH A "TUBA" PASTE

27. **Jumbles:** NIECE DUNCE TACKLE SWERVE
    Answer: A guy who works at this doesn't have much chance of getting ahead—INTERVALS

28. **Jumbles:** BEGUN JADED SKEWER NICELY
    Answer: What a green thumb can mean for a professional gardener—"GREENBACKS"

29. **Jumbles:** CURVE BERTH ENZYME HARROW
    Answer: What the male sheep shouted in order to get his mate's attention—"HEY, EWE"

30. **Jumbles:** HUSKY CAMEO JOYFUL HEALTH
    Answer: When a coward gets into a "jam," you can expect him to do this—SHAKE LIKE JELLY

31. **Jumbles:** FOIST CHAMP SNUGLY MYSTIC
    Answer: What the misogynist felt he had in the world—A "MISS-SHUN"

32. **Jumbles:** ABASH HYENA SWIVEL DAMASK
    Answer: Strong lungs often appeal to people with this—WEAK HEADS

33. **Jumbles:** ABBEY CHOKE VOLUME GUTTER
    Answer: Age may be the difference between these—A CURVE & A BULGE

34. **Jumbles:** REARM EMERY BEHOLD STODGY
    Answer: A comfortable old shoe might be this, through thick and thin—YOUR "SOLE" MATE

35. **Jumbles:** AUDIT EXPEL BICEPS UNLOAD
    Answer: When gossip is at its most malicious, they sometimes relish it as this—"DELICIOUS"

36. **Jumbles:** CEASE FLOUR RARELY INFIRM
    Answer: The curve that usually sets things straight—A SMILE

37. **Jumbles:** GUEST PLUSH SURELY IRONIC
    Answer: What a crooked politician with a "knotty" problem might try to do—PULL STRINGS

38. **Jumbles:** AORTA BUILT MALADY FILLET
    Answer: Words of praise that seldom fall flat—FLATTERY

39. **Jumbles:** EXERT FACET QUORUM TURNIP
    Answer: Why you should study the history of the past—THERE'S A FUTURE IN IT

40. **Jumbles:** METAL CUBIT SHADOW KILLER
    Answer: What he would do every time he saw the girl at the candy counter—SWEET-TALK HER

41. **Jumbles:** CLEFT BRIBE DEFILE INTACT
    Answer: The egotist's love letter—THE LETTER "I"

42. **Jumbles:** GROIN DINER COERCE FIESTA
    Answer: When the skunk entered the room it got attention because it was this—THE "SCENTER" OF IT

43. **Jumbles:** WOMEN PANSY CORNEA BICKER
    Answer: Where the deposits are "frozen assets"—IN A "SNOW BANK"

44. **Jumbles:** ELATE MINUS SPLEEN NUDISM
    Answer: The nervous tailor was always on this—PINS & NEEDLES

45. **Jumbles:** IVORY FIORD SHANTY DEFACE
Answer: That well-dressed woman was indeed a credit to her husband, thanks to this—HIS CREDIT

46. **Jumbles:** BRAVE ERASE UNPAID CLOUDY
Answer: When you call the plumber because of a leak it might end up being this—A DRAIN ON YOU

47. **Jumbles:** NEEDY BARON SECEDE ELDEST
Answer: The judge's words were less important than this—HIS SENTENCES

48. **Jumbles:** PROVE SHEEP INFUSE MANIAC
Answer: What an employee has if he laughs at the boss's jokes even when they make no this—"SENSE"

49. **Jumbles:** OAKEN FAITH PREACH CUPFUL
Answer: Could it be head covering for a traveler to the Arctic?—A POLAR ICE "CAP"

50. **Jumbles:** GRAIN ITCHY MELODY VASSAL
Answer: What happened when their shellfish business suffered financial reverses—IT WAS A "CLAM-ITY"

51. **Jumbles:** RURAL VILLA BUSHEL WATERY
Answer: He married a woman who could indeed take a joke—HE WAS IT!

52. **Jumbles:** IVORY CRANK DISCUS KIDNAP
Answer: Some men don't like being ordered around unless it's this—A ROUND OF DRINKS

53. **Jumbles:** SUAVE BOUGH GENTLE CROTCH
Answer: A person who leaves too much to chance hasn't—GOT A CHANCE

54. **Jumbles:** SKIMP EXPEL ACCENT DAMPEN
Answer: What the hosts said, when their welcome was outstayed by a guest—"PEST!"

55. **Jumbles:** AROMA CABIN MORGUE TAUGHT
Answer: That fortune-hunting bachelor said he was never going to marry until he found this—THE RIGHT AMOUNT

56. **Jumbles:** BARGE AISLE DRAGON PESTLE
Answer: What a person who has failed to keep up his payments on the car is called—A PEDESTRIAN

57. **Jumbles:** GRAVE BROIL IRONIC MODIFY
Answer: Something in a hat store that might make you look foolish—A MIRROR

58. **Jumbles:** IDIOT BERTH POLISH AMBUSH
Answer: When neighbors gossip over a fence, there's much to be said—ON BOTH SIDES

59. **Jumbles:** IMPEL DOILY JERSEY INLAND
Answer: A person who is constantly giving others a piece of his mind usually has this—NONE TO SPARE

60. **Jumbles:** OWING SOOTY POTTER NEARBY
Answer: A single word that may take the place of a long sentence—"PROBATION"

61. **Jumbles:** FRANC LADLE DISMAL NICELY
Answer: The egocentric is seldom concerned about ideals, but always with—"I" DEALS

62. **Jumbles:** OCTET ABATE EMPLOY TURNIP
Answer: What a successful headwaiter is—"TIP-TOP"

63. **Jumbles:** FABLE BASSO STOLEN GENDER
Answer: What that eloquent criminal lawyer used on the jury—"TEAR GAS"

64. **Jumbles:** JUMPY ADULT HEALTH UPWARD
Answer: What the chairman of the meeting did to get such rapt attention—RAPPED

65. **Jumbles:** DAUNT UNCAP SUBMIT WHITEN
Answer: That hobo was always down and out but never this—"WASHED UP"

66. **Jumbles:** GAUZE ICILY LOTION INVERT
Answer: What kind of wire makes the best "connections"?—A "LIVE" ONE

67. **Jumbles:** FLUTE VIXEN TRUANT PREACH
Answer: The best way to make a long story short—INTERRUPT HIM

68. **Jumbles:** MINUS TITLE SPLEEN FAMISH
Answer: Where the prevaricator's character lies—IN HIS LIES

69. **Jumbles:** GIANT BASIN OBTUSE TALLOW
Answer: Often drunk but never intoxicated—A TOAST

70. **Jumbles:** WHILE SWOOP KERNEL SIPHON
Answer: When the dentist does work on your teeth, it often provides—WORK FOR HIS OWN

71. **Jumbles:** REARM DADDY EXEMPT MENACE
Answer: What he took after every meal in order to get his weight down—A NAP

72. **Jumbles:** BOOTY FINIS STUCCO PELVIS
Answer: What it takes to keep a lawyer well-dressed—A LOT OF SUITS

73. **Jumbles:** FLAKE ROBOT GENIUS WINTRY
Answer: A flatterer always says the right thing for this—THE WRONG REASON

74. **Jumbles:** AUDIT CHAMP KILLER SOCIAL
Answer: Could be the mark of a great lover—LIPSTICK

75. **Jumbles:** ODIUM ANKLE BYGONE DIGEST
Answer: How spring often comes—"SODDEN-LY"

76. **Jumbles:** MERCY PHOTO MOSQUE SICKEN
Answer: Where the investment banker turned actor could regularly be seen—IN SUMMER "STOCK"

77. **Jumbles:** ELEGY PANIC BOUNCE FABRIC
Answer: Another name for all that baggage that goes into the vehicle—"CAR-GO"

78. **Jumbles:** TEMPO BLOOD MARVEL EMPIRE
Answer: What a skilled gardener knows how to do—IMPROVE HIS "LOT"

79. **Jumbles:** MANLY ENVOY CHORUS DIVIDE
Answer: In some businesses it's not the overhead but this—THE UNDERHAND

80. **Jumbles:** CAMEO FATAL DARING BOILED
Answer: What a parent's major problem sometimes is—A MINOR

81. **Jumbles:** BRAVE LITHE MEADOW PURPLE
Answer: What the chronic procrastinator had—A "WAIT" PROBLEM

82. **Jumbles:** SAUTE DRYLY CUPFUL PLURAL
Answer: What they call a lot of crumbs held together by their own dough—THE UPPER CRUST

83. **Jumbles:** EPOCH AFTER FASTEN MALICE
Answer: A self-indulgent guy never does this—"NO" HIMSELF

84. **Jumbles:** ABHOR FOCUS PARISH LACKEY
Answer: She knew her husband like a book—A "SCRAP" BOOK

85. **Jumbles:** EXERT RAINY DOMINO SCARCE
Answer: Many a woman thinks she is fond of sports until she does this—MARRIES ONE

86. **Jumbles:** FUDGE AGILE BUCKLE CRAYON
Answer: What happens when automobiles are so close together they can't move—GRIDLOCK

87. **Jumbles:** DOUSE JUMBO EXPEND FACTOR
Answer: What that expensive toupee got him—IN DEBT OVER HIS EARS

88. **Jumbles:** PAUSE TEPID CIPHER NUANCE
Answer: Lots of "pull" will get you almost anywhere, except when this is required—"PUSH"

89. **Jumbles:** DUNCE AMUSE LETHAL SADIST
Answer: What those neighborhood busybodies belonged to—THE "MEDDLE" CLASS

90. **Jumbles:** BOUND ELOPE DELUGE FORMAT
Answer: What the rug merchant's jokes did—FLOORED 'EM

91. **Jumbles:** DRONE HEDGE BROOCH HOURLY
Answer: What the baker turned comedian knew how to make—DOUGH OUT OF "CORN"

92. **Jumbles:** DEITY PAPER CAVORT MODIFY
Answer: His lifework was to—AVOID IT

185

93. **Jumbles:** PROVE METAL FETISH SHANTY
Answer: What they call that guy who always remains at a party after the food and drink are all gone—THE HOST

94. **Jumbles:** ALBUM GRAVE BRUTAL RAGLAN
Answer: What the bachelor's views were—"UN-ALTAR-ABLE"

95. **Jumbles:** GOING ALTAR BARREL LAWYER
Answer: What "little white lies" usually are—YELLOW

96. **Jumbles:** FANCY LIMBO PUSHER KETTLE
Answer: What Congress passed when they couldn't think of any new laws—THE BUCK

97. **Jumbles:** GORGE FAIRY DEMISE BUCKET
Answer: Often when you save up for a rainy day you end up getting this—"SOAKED"

98. **Jumbles:** FINAL RAPID WOBBLE INHALE
Answer: Where a businessman who's always "on the level" shouldn't have to go—DOWNHILL

99. **Jumbles:** HEAVY JUICE WEASEL SWIVEL
Answer: What there was in the courthouse—MORE "JAW" THAN LAW

100. **Jumbles:** BRIBE LATCH ABRUPT UNWISE
Answer: Where the snobs lived—IN "SNUBURBIA"

101. **Jumbles:** DECRY MAUVE BANISH FORGET
Answer: Water power that helps run many households—TEARS

102. **Jumbles:** BEIGE FEVER SCHOOL FIERCE
Answer: Those noisy neighbors thought they were enjoying the right of—FREE "SCREECH"

103. **Jumbles:** HASTY LAPEL FEWEST POLICE
Answer: What she said to her overly-friendly dancing partner—"WATCH YOUR STEP"

104. **Jumbles:** FLOUR PIETY MALADY TERROR
Answer: He wasn't contented with his lot—always asking for this—A LOT MORE

105. **Jumbles:** GLOVE HIKER CANINE BOUGHT
Answer: What the nudist camp's star athlete ran a hundred yards in—NOTHING

106. **Jumbles:** MAKER COUGH TRIBAL HARROW
Answer: As she did this, words passed between them—THREW THE BOOK AT HIM

107. **Jumbles:** PECAN LIBEL UNLESS BOTHER
Answer: Whoever said that money grows on trees didn't know that you've also got to—BEAT THE BUSHES FOR IT

108. **Jumbles:** ARMOR CANAL RATION LAUNCH
Answer: How most things are sold in a supermarket—À LA "CART"

109. **Jumbles:** BISON LINER JACKET PICNIC
Answer: What's the only illness you can catch from a hypochondriac?—A PAIN IN THE NECK

110. **Jumbles:** STOOP QUAIL PIGEON GOPHER
Answer: How to find out what's up—GO SHOPPING

111. **Jumbles:** ONION TIPSY PANTRY MINGLE
Answer: When challenged to deliver such a huge bouquet for the special occasion, the florist—ROSE TO IT

112. **Jumbles:** MOTTO HONEY TONGUE VENDOR
Answer: When Michael Collins piloted the Apollo 11 command module on 7-21-69, he was—OVER THE MOON

113. **Jumbles:** NUDGE PROVE IODINE SCROLL
Answer: When the Viking leader needed a new means of communication, he invented—"NORSE" CODE

114. **Jumbles:** UNFIT ALLOW SECEDE TIGHTS
Answer: When it came to making balloon animals, this guy had an—INFLATED EGO

115. **Jumbles:** SHINY DIGIT AWAKEN COUGAR
Answer: Daffy Duck was retiring and he took the duck replacing him—UNDER HIS WING

116. **Jumbles:** EPOXY IMPEL TURKEY ABACUS
Answer: When it came to buying the right glue for their model airplane, his father was being a—STICKLER

117. **Jumbles:** BISON TENTH EASILY LAWMAN
Answer: The ping-pong playing horses were enjoying their game of—"STABLE" TENNIS

118. **Jumbles:** EAGLE QUAKE BESIDE NOTIFY
Answer: The twins who worked for the spy agency were—DOUBLE AGENTS

119. **Jumbles:** SPOIL EJECT SOCIAL ORNERY
Answer: The forest of scissors had—"PAIR" TREES

120. **Jumbles:** FLOWN SLANT EMBARK COGNAC
Answer: The family loved their new kitten. Everyone thought she was the—CAT'S MEOW

121. **Jumbles:** CHIRP ALBUM UNPACK PLAGUE
Answer: She had her friend drive her to the coffee shop because she needed a—PICK-ME-UP

122. **Jumbles:** SHOVE SWIFT HIGHLY ANYHOW
Answer: She just couldn't decide if she was going to do the laundry. She was being—WISHY-WASHY

123. **Jumbles:** ALPHA SILKY GOALIE REVERE
Answer: After chopping firewood all day, he was going to—SLEEP LIKE A LOG

124. **Jumbles:** COLOR TOTAL HECKLE ASYLUM
Answer: The fisherman threw the little fish back and said—CATCH YOU LATER

125. **Jumbles:** RATIO DERBY SHODDY HEAVEN
Answer: When the U.S. president jumped the stallion over the fence, he rode on—AIR "HORSE" ONE

126. **Jumbles:** WHILE ELDER INFAMY TOMCAT
Answer: The pickpocket at the bottom of the Grand Canyon was a—LOWLIFE

127. **Jumbles:** AGAIN CHORD UTMOST SWIVEL
Answer: Thomas Edison was able to invent the phonograph, thanks to the fact that his—LOGIC WAS SOUND

128. **Jumbles:** MAUVE NAVAL BEMOAN ATRIUM
Answer: The tightrope walker who stopped to check his e-mail was—ONLINE

129. **Jumbles:** QUERY MOVIE CENSUS NEATLY
Answer: He needed a partner to build a new abacus business, and his buddy said—COUNT ME IN

130. **Jumbles:** GOING BRAVO WEAPON COMEDY
Answer: The plant nursery owners' son was a—GROWING BOY

131. **Jumbles:** RUGBY SCOUR COBWEB DEADLY
Answer: When they asked Robin Hood if he'd like to have their next meeting in the forest, he said he—SURE WOULD

132. **Jumbles:** GRIPE HOUND TENANT SCENIC
Answer: He wasn't favored to win the marathon, but he was —IN THE RUNNING

133. **Jumbles:** BRASH KIOSK CHANGE WALRUS
Answer: The instructor for the job training course taught the—WORKING CLASS

134. **Jumbles:** COVET DRAWN COWARD GALLEY
Answer: He thought the zombies wouldn't attack. He would end up being—DEAD WRONG

135. **Jumbles:** RIGID THINK STIGMA SHRIMP
Answer: When the ghosts reached the top of the mountain, they were—IN HIGH SPIRITS

136. **Jumbles:** NACHO AGENT VORTEX EYELID
Answer: The Tower of Pisa's building inspectors were—TOO "LEAN"-IENT

137. **Jumbles:** PROUD GRIME ENTICE CHUNKY
Answer: The used album store would eventually go out of business due to its poor—RECORD KEEPING

138. **Jumbles:** AVIAN MADLY REJECT LOATHE
Answer: When the twins played tennis, they were—EVENLY MATCHED

139. **Jumbles:** ABATE ODDLY WINNER ADJUST
Answer: The pilot quit because he wanted to—LAND A NEW JOB

140. **Jumbles:** MONEY TRACT REMOVE MAYHEM
Answer: When she thought her daughter might have a fever, she used her—"THERM-MOM-METER"

141. **Jumbles:** HIKER ROBOT INVITE OUTAGE
Answer: He broke his wife's favorite figurine, and now he had to—BREAK IT TO HER

142. **Jumbles:** LEAKY MILKY NORMAL TURNIP
Answer: The fabric she'd use to make a new dress was—IMMATERIAL

143. **Jumbles:** BRAVO LIMIT MIDDAY UNLESS
Answer: Following his friend's advice instead of seeing his doctor was—ILL-ADVISED

144. **Jumbles:** SEIZE RELIC UNRULY TUXEDO
Answer: The fisherman thought he'd hooked a huge one. It didn't take long until he was—"REEL" SURE

145. **Jumbles:** APART KHAKI FUNGUS PELLET
Answer: To refuel the armored combat vehicle, they needed to—FILL UP THE TANK

146. **Jumbles:** DIZZY HONOR FITTED GIGGLE
Answer: After he bit into the tasty frankfurter, he said—HOT DIGGITY DOG!

147. **Jumbles:** GAUGE ALIAS THROWN SOCIAL
Answer: The carpenter has had his hammer for so long because it was—TOUGH AS NAILS

148. **Jumbles:** TRUCK AMAZE ACCENT PEOPLE
Answer: After getting into an accident, her new Mercedes was a—COMPACT CAR

149. **Jumbles:** BYLAW AFTER BOLDLY SESAME
Answer: The sponge came to life and could now talk. Too bad he was so—SELF-ABSORBED

150. **Jumbles:** GLADE MERGE LOUNGE WORTHY
Answer: The bride was beautiful and her husband-to-be was—WELL-GROOMED

151. **Jumbles:** BRASH DRAWN ENTICE HICCUP
Answer: When the economy expands, the number of new job openings goes—"HIRE" AND "HIRE"

152. **Jumbles:** HEFTY BURST THIRST APPEAR
Answer: When his wife made cake mix for the baseball player, he said—BATTER UP

153. **Jumbles:** HEAVY TAUNT ZODIAC ARCADE
Answer: Her official biography would be written by the writer she—"AUTHOR-IZED"

154. **Jumbles:** KNIFE NOVEL GROUCH CAVIAR
Answer: Having too much garbage in the landfill was—REEKING HAVOC

155. **Jumbles:** IMPEL WEIGH CANOPY GROWTH
Answer: When they got back home, their dogs greeted them with a—WELCOME "WAGGIN'"

156. **Jumbles:** ONION FRONT MAYHEM SUBDUE
Answer: Before in-ear digital hearing aids were invented, they were—UNHEARD OF

157. **Jumbles:** STYLE GRIME IRONIC BARREL
Answer: The airport had to be torn down because its problems were—TERMINAL

158. **Jumbles:** RODEO SHYLY TOPPLE RITUAL
Answer: The fast-growing trees were selling very quickly because they were—SO "POPLAR"

159. **Jumbles:** LUCKY OZONE ENTITY DIVINE
Answer: His wife wanted to hike up the hill, but he wasn't—INCLINED TO

160. **Jumbles:** DRAFT PETTY INJECT SQUAWK
Answer: She bought the restaurant, but the food would be an—ACQUIRED TASTE

161. **Jumbles:** AUHOR DISMAL BUCKLE LUNACY FIDDLE EMERGE
Answer: There was no skullduggery involved here—just this—"SCULL-DRUDGERY"

162. **Jumbles:** CLERGY FATHOM JINGLE AMBUSH PAUNCH DARING
Answer: What you might see in a seafood restaurant—A "MAN EATING FISH"

163. **Jumbles:** INVADE DAMAGE ASSAIL MOTHER SWIVEL FORCED
Answer: The burglars managed to get everything except this—WHAT'S COMING TO THEM

164. **Jumbles:** TURKEY AUBURN EXEMPT SPEEDY UPWARD BUZZER
Answer: What Julius Caesar probably knew when he devised his calendar—THAT HIS DAYS WERE "NUMBERED"

165. **Jumbles:** RAVAGE VOLUME DROWSY NEEDLE OUTLAW THRUSH
Answer: He pretended to be performing that famous trick, but the audience found it this—HARD TO SWALLOW

166. **Jumbles:** POLITE BOLERO WORTHY TWINGE UTMOST CLOTHE
Answer: Elephants live so long because they never worry about this—HOW TO LOSE WEIGHT

167. **Jumbles:** ERMINE ARTFUL ISLAND BROKER OBLONG ELDEST
Answer: How the intruder got into the house—"IN-TRU-DER" DOOR (in through the door)

168. **Jumbles:** BISHOP AFFIRM CHROME STRONG AUTUMN UNSOLD
Answer: What the members of that famous "think tank" usually enjoyed —"FOOD" FOR THOUGHT

169. **Jumbles:** LOCALE THRESH CROUCH ANYWAY PERMIT TRUDGE
Answer: Why the skeleton was afraid to jump off—HE HAD NO GUTS

170. **Jumbles:** CHALET BELLOW DAINTY MATRON GAIETY THEORY
Answer: What people need before they can build a big house—A WHOLE LOT

171. **Jumbles:** DREDGE SHRIMP ALWAYS SCRIPT CANYON POLISH
Answer: To compete in the poker tournament, her husband would need to—PLAY HIS CARDS RIGHT

172. **Jumbles:** UNLOCK BUDGET IMPOSE UNEASY MENACE PRIMER
Answer: Thanks to his fleet of garbage trucks, the business owner had—DISPOSABLE INCOME

173. **Jumbles:** TWENTY VENDOR SMOKER INJECT EMERGE INHALE
Answer: She was going to bring the sugar cookies with her so she could—TAKE HER SWEET TIME

174. **Jumbles:** SCORCH SMOOCH IGUANA OBLONG MOTIVE ELICIT
Answer: With so many of her children there, Mother's Day was a—"MOM-ENTOUS" OCCASION

175. **Jumbles:** SUMMER UPDATE NEGATE IMPALA BEACON OFFEND
Answer: When Mount Rushmore was completed, people came from all over to see the—LAND "FOUR-MATION"

176. **Jumbles:** INFORM HOLLOW TAMPER ENOUGH HELMET SWITCH
Answer: He hadn't won the Indy 500 yet, but the—WHEELS WERE IN MOTION

177. **Jumbles:** IMMUNE HUDDLE FRIGHT POETRY FIBBER PARLOR
Answer: He liked driving cars with his sister at the amusement park where traffic was—"BUMP-HER" TO "BUMP-HER"

178. **Jumbles:** FORGET SPRAWL FABRIC DEVOUT EASILY DOUBLE
Answer: The cows started patrolling the cattle ranch after deciding they needed to—BEEF UP SECURITY

179. **Jumbles:** UPBEAT BECKON AVENUE YELLOW UPHILL CACTUS
Answer: The new dad was exhausted, so for Father's Day, his wife let him—SLEEP LIKE A BABY

180. **Jumbles:** VANITY SLEEPY OPPOSE CLINIC VERBAL ACTUAL
Answer: The fraudulent computer programmers lived in—"SILLY-CON" VALLEY

Need More Jumbles®?

Jumble® Books

More than 175 puzzles each!

Cowboy Jumble®
$9.95 • ISBN: 978-1-62937-355-3

Jammin' Jumble®
$9.95 • ISBN: 1-57243-844-4

Java Jumble®
$9.95 • ISBN: 978-1-60078-415-6

Jazzy Jumble®
$9.95 • ISBN: 978-1-57243-962-7

Jet Set Jumble®
$9.95 • ISBN: 978-1-60078-353-1

Joyful Jumble®
$9.95 • ISBN: 978-1-60078-079-0

Juke Joint Jumble®
$9.95 • ISBN: 978-1-60078-295-4

Jumble® Anniversary
$10.95 • ISBN: 987-1-62937-734-6

Jumble® at Work
$9.95 • ISBN: 1-57243-147-4

Jumble® Ballet
$10.95 • ISBN: 978-1-62937-616-5

Jumble® Birthday
$10.95 • ISBN: 978-1-62937-652-3

Jumble® Celebration
$9.95 • ISBN: 978-1-60078-134-6

Jumble® Circus
$9.95 • ISBN: 978-1-60078-739-3

Jumble® Cuisine
$10.95 • ISBN: 978-1-62937-735-3

Jumble® Drag Race
$9.95 • ISBN: 978-1-62937-483-3

Jumble® Ever After
$10.95 • ISBN: 978-1-62937-785-8

Jumble® Explorer
$9.95 • ISBN: 978-1-60078-854-3

Jumble® Explosion
$9.95 • ISBN: 978-1-60078-078-3

Jumble® Fever
$9.95 • ISBN: 1-57243-593-3

Jumble® Fiesta
$9.95 • ISBN: 1-57243-626-3

Jumble® Fun
$9.95 • ISBN: 1-57243-379-5

Jumble® Galaxy
$9.95 • ISBN: 978-1-60078-583-2

Jumble® Garden
$10.95 • ISBN: 978-1-62937-653-0

Jumble® Genius
$9.95 • ISBN: 1-57243-896-7

Jumble® Geography
$10.95 • ISBN: 978-1-62937-615-8

Jumble® Getaway
$9.95 • ISBN: 978-1-60078-547-4

Jumble® Gold
$9.95 • ISBN: 978-1-62937-354-6

Jumble® Grab Bag
$9.95 • ISBN: 1-57243-273-X

Jumble® Gymnastics
$9.95 • ISBN: 978-1-62937-306-5

Jumble® Jackpot
$9.95 • ISBN: 1-57243-897-5

Jumble® Jailbreak
$9.95 • ISBN: 978-1-62937-002-6

Jumble® Jambalaya
$9.95 • ISBN: 978-1-60078-294-7

Jumble® Jamboree
$9.95 • ISBN: 1-57243-696-4

Jumble® Jitterbug
$9.95 • ISBN: 978-1-60078-584-9

Jumble® Journey
$9.95 • ISBN: 978-1-62937-549-6

Jumble® Jubilation
$10.95 • ISBN: 978-1-62937-784-1

Jumble® Jubilee
$9.95 • ISBN: 1-57243-231-4

Jumble® Juggernaut
$9.95 • ISBN: 978-1-60078-026-4

Jumble® Junction
$9.95 • ISBN: 1-57243-380-9

Jumble® Jungle
$9.95 • ISBN: 978-1-57243-961-0

Jumble® Kingdom
$9.95 • ISBN: 978-1-62937-079-8

Jumble® Knockout
$9.95 • ISBN: 978-1-62937-078-1

Jumble® Madness
$9.95 • ISBN: 1-892049-24-4

Jumble® Magic
$9.95 • ISBN: 978-1-60078-795-9

Jumble® Marathon
$9.95 • ISBN: 978-1-62937-548-9

Jumble® Parachute
$9.95 • ISBN: 978-1-60078-944-1

Jumble® Safari
$9.95 • ISBN: 978-1-60078-675-4

Jumble® See & Search
$9.95 • ISBN: 1-57243-549-6

Jumble® See & Search 2
$9.95 • ISBN: 1-57243-734-0

Jumble® Sensation
$9.95 • ISBN: 978-1-60078-548-1

Jumble® Surprise
$9.95 • ISBN: 1-57243-320-5

Jumble® Symphony
$9.95 • ISBN: 978-1-62937-131-3

Jumble® Theater
$9.95 • ISBN: 978-1-62937-484-03

Jumble® University
$9.95 • ISBN: 978-1-62937-001-9

Jumble® Vacation
$9.95 • ISBN: 978-1-60078-796-6

Jumble® Wedding
$9.95 • ISBN: 978-1-62937-307-2

Jumble® Workout
$9.95 • ISBN: 978-1-60078-943-4

Jumpin' Jumble®
$9.95 • ISBN: 978-1-60078-027-1

Lunar Jumble®
$9.95 • ISBN: 978-1-60078-853-6

Monster Jumble®
$9.95 • ISBN: 978-1-62937-213-6

Mystic Jumble®
$9.95 • ISBN: 978-1-62937-130-6

Outer Space Jumble®
$9.95 • ISBN: 978-1-60078-416-3

Rainy Day Jumble®
$9.95 • ISBN: 978-1-60078-352-4

Ready, Set, Jumble®
$9.95 • ISBN: 978-1-60078-133-0

Rock 'n' Roll Jumble®
$9.95 • ISBN: 978-1-60078-674-7

Royal Jumble®
$9.95 • ISBN: 978-1-60078-738-6

Sports Jumble®
$9.95 • ISBN: 1-57243-113-X

Summer Fun Jumble®
$9.95 • ISBN: 1-57243-114-8

Touchdown Jumble®
$9.95 • ISBN: 978-1-62937-212-9

Travel Jumble®
$9.95 • ISBN: 1-57243-198-9

TV Jumble®
$9.95 • ISBN: 1-57243-461-9

Oversize Jumble® Books

More than 500 puzzles each!

Generous Jumble®
$19.95 • ISBN: 1-57243-385-X

Giant Jumble®
$19.95 • ISBN: 1-57243-349-3

Gigantic Jumble®
$19.95 • ISBN: 1-57243-426-0

Jumbo Jumble®
$19.95 • ISBN: 1-57243-314-0

The Very Best of Jumble® BrainBusters
$19.95 • ISBN: 1-57243-845-2

Jumble® Crosswords™

More than 175 puzzles each!

More Jumble® Crosswords™
$9.95 • ISBN: 1-57243-386-8

Jumble® Crosswords™ Jackpot
$9.95 • ISBN: 1-57243-615-8

Jumble® Crosswords™ Jamboree
$9.95 • ISBN: 1-57243-787-1

Jumble® BrainBusters™

More than 175 puzzles each!

Jumble® BrainBusters™
$9.95 • ISBN: 1-892049-28-7

Jumble® BrainBusters™ II
$9.95 • ISBN: 1-57243-424-4

Jumble® BrainBusters™ III
$9.95 • ISBN: 1-57243-463-5

Jumble® BrainBusters™ IV
$9.95 • ISBN: 1-57243-489-9

Jumble® BrainBusters™ 5
$9.95 • ISBN: 1-57243-548-8

Jumble® BrainBusters™ Bonanza
$9.95 • ISBN: 1-57243-616-6

Boggle™ BrainBusters™
$9.95 • ISBN: 1-57243-592-5

Boggle™ BrainBusters™ 2
$9.95 • ISBN: 1-57243-788-X

Jumble® BrainBusters™ Junior
$9.95 • ISBN: 1-892049-29-5

Jumble® BrainBusters™ Junior II
$9.95 • ISBN: 1-57243-425-2

Fun in the Sun with Jumble® BrainBusters™
$9.95 • ISBN: 1-57243-733-2